MW01153517

THE CHICAGO BUNGALOW

THE CHICAGO BUNGALOW

CHICAGO ARCHITECTURE FOUNDATION

Dominic A. Pacyga & Charles Shanabruch
CO-EDITORS

Mati Maldre
CONTEMPORARY PHOTOGRAPHY

ARCADIA

Copyright © 2001 by The Chicago Architecture Foundation.
Photographic Copyright © 2001 by Mati Maldre.

First Printed 2001.
Reprinted 2002.

ISBN 0-7385-1882-4

Edited by Dominic A. Pacyga and Charles Shanabruch.
Contemporary Architectural Photography by Mati Maldre.

Published by Arcadia Publishing,
an imprint of Tempus Publishing, Inc.
3047 N. Lincoln Ave., Suite 410
Chicago, IL 60657

Printed in Great Britain.

Library of Congress Catalog Card Number 2001093285

For all general information contact Arcadia Publishing at:
Telephone 843-853-2070
Fax 843-853-0044
E-Mail sales@arcadiapublishing.com

For customer service and orders:
Toll-Free 1-888-313-2665

Visit us on the internet at http://www.arcadiapublishing.com

CONTENTS

This bungalow on South Lowe Street in Chicago's Bridgeport neighborhood is perhaps the city's most famous residence. Here the late Mayor Richard J. Daley and his wife raised their family. Mrs. Daley continues to reside in the home. (Photograph by Mati Maldre.)

PREFACE

Chicago is world-renowned for great architecture: Frank Lloyd Wright, Louis Sullivan, and a host of other innovative architects each built their reputations here. Yet the Chicago architectural contribution most common in the city is one that is attached to no particular architect or single home but to thousands of them—the Chicago Bungalow. Built in the early 1900s, with their detailed windows, stone work, pitched roofs, sheltered entrances, and neat lawns, the bungalow became immediately popular. For the first time, average Chicagoans could be homeowners as dignified housing for all was available at modest cost. The 80,000 to 100,000 bungalows built between 1910 and 1940 stood as visible proof of the increasing prosperity of Chicago's working families.

Chicago Bungalows are as stalwart as Chicagoans, withstanding winter after frigid winter. Their brick construction and one-and-one-half-story profile, which lend a hunkered-down look on cold snowy days, have protected residents from the elements for generations. But they also allow for the full enjoyment of Chicago's precious warm-weather months, too; some still have the window box brackets and lovely planters that originally graced them.

This book is a celebration not only of bungalow architecture in Chicago but of the homes' diverse residents and neighborhoods as well. Adding to the fabric of each neighborhood are local houses of worship, parks, and other cultural keystones. It explores the origins, building, finance, and the special place of the bungalow in women's domestic history. From early evolution of the city's Bungalow Belt to the present, Chicago Bungalow communities cover the full ethnic, racial, economic, and generational spectrum.

Chicago's bungalows and Bungalow Belt neighborhoods are as attractive to homebuyers today as when they were in the vanguard of urban housing. They are an architectural treasure and critical part of the city's housing infrastructure—comprising nearly a third of Chicago's single-family housing. The city's Historic Chicago Bungalow Initiative was set forth to provide an education, financing, and marketing program to celebrate the architectural and historical importance and to ensure the viability of the Chicago Bungalow's contribution to families, neighborhoods, and the nation's architecture. This project was initiated by the City of Chicago's Department of Housing, and is a joint endeavor of the City of Chicago, the Chicago Architecture Foundation, and the newly created Historic Chicago Bungalow Association.

All this may seem like a lot of attention on the humble Chicago Bungalow. It is, and it is well deserved. Indeed, the Chicago Bungalow is a Chicago icon.

Bonita C. Mall
Chicago Architecture Foundation

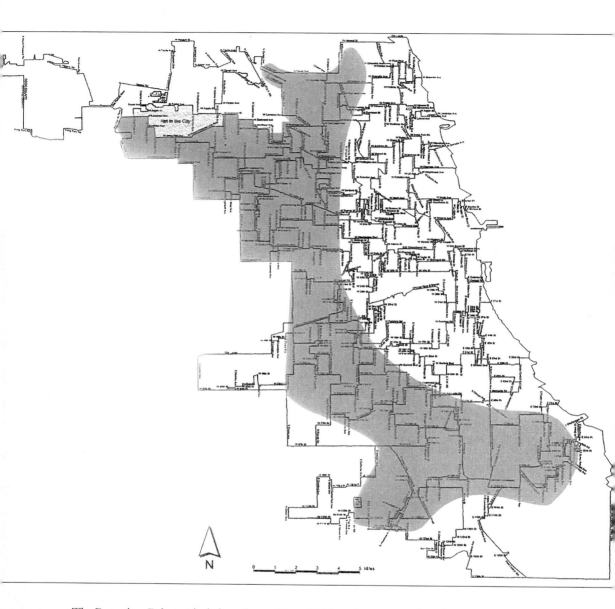

The Bungalow Belt stretched along the outskirts of Chicago in a crescent shape between the suburbs and the industrial neighborhoods outside the Loop. (Courtesy of City of Chicago Department of Housing.)

one

DEFINING
THE CHICAGO BUNGALOW

by Scott Sonoc

Nearly 80,000 bungalows line Chicago's streets and in many neighborhoods are the dominant housing type. While these homes may appear the same, a close look will reveal many differences that created a sense of individuality for the owner. (Photograph by Mati Maldre.)

I t is difficult if not impossible to design without an awareness of the prevailing "zeitgeist" or "spirit" of the time in which we live. The architects who gave shape to the Chicago Bungalow did so as a result of the concurrence of influences between 1880 and 1940. These included various cultural, economic, technical, and social concepts. The "zeitgeist" of the late 1800s included the American desire to create an architecture that reflected a new way of life, different from old European influences. The young free enterprise system was being quickly pushed along by a growing population and plenty of cheap land to develop. As well, the conveniences of time-saving mass-produced products and the demands from a more educated urban population predicated the formation of a new lifestyle with new housing demands.

In 1926, a high school home economics textbook, *The House and Its Care*, described what a residence should look like, how it should function, and how it should be maintained. Concerning a house's appearance, the book states,

> . . . *To secure a good architectural composition it is essential to achieve both 'unity' and 'balance.' 'Unity' means the arrangement of different parts in such a way as to produce a harmonious whole, while 'balance' means an arrangement which makes the general proportions of the building pleasing.*

> . . . *A well designed house expresses sincerity through simple lines, the use of good material, and the avoidance of all shams; it expresses beauty through good proportion, pleasing decoration, and a balance of parts; it emphasizes purpose, through an arrangement of rooms, to be of greatest comfort and convenience to all members of the family.*

Today, as in the late 1800s and early 1900s, architects strive to artfully create houses by manipulating lines, planes, curves, and colors, vying to add sculptural and visual beauty to the world. Architects are taught to create as artists with toolboxes filled with abstract shapes. Depending on how the pieces are put together, an entire house and even small parts of a house can display specific characteristics and maybe even exhibit an idea or a notion to evoke a memory or tell a story. The architectural character of a bungalow in Chicago can be discovered by looking back past the early twentieth century and watching how the pertinent issues of those days influenced the architects' designs, as it is those architectural designs that would ultimately culminate in the Chicago Bungalow.

CHICAGO BUNGALOW ORIGINS

As the population in the United States spread across the land, the need to build housing fast and economically became the rule of the day. In the nineteenth century, railroads expanded rapidly across the continent providing transportation and creating a national market. Manufacturing companies began to mass produce building products in standardized shapes and sizes, like nails and thin lumber for "Balloon Frame Construction." Prior to manufactured building products, skilled carpenters crafted homes out of local materials, as with log cabin and traditional hand cut timber techniques.

Between 1871 and 1900, the predominant residential building style in Chicago was "Victorian." Many regional variations, all within the Victorian style, were overlaid as character themes to generate residential building variety. These themes included "French-Mansard," "Stick Style," "Shingle," and "Romanesque."

From 1880 to 1920, the City of Chicago annexed surrounding farmland and suburbs. New infrastructure was being installed, including streets and alleys, water and sewer pipes, gas pipes, electric lines, and public rail transportation. Developers transformed rural land into new neighborhoods.

As streetcar lines and later automobiles helped people get to jobs more quickly, the need to live close to work became less of a necessity. In fact, because Chicago's population had grown so quickly during the late 1800s, downtown neighborhoods became overburdened with too many people and too little infrastructure. Apartment buildings and two-flats quickly crowded the city's residential areas. Residential densities in Chicago typically ranged from 28 to 40 units per acre in the older inner-city neighborhoods built before 1900. Afterwards, the block and alley patterns remained essentially the same, yet residential densities of 10 to 12 units per acre dominated in newer neighborhoods.

Aware of the unsanitary and threatening conditions in which many children lived in Chicago's neighborhoods, social reformer Jane Addams stressed the importance of raising

Streetcars such as these at 79th Street and Exchange Avenue were essential to the development of the Bungalow Belt in Chicago. They made it possible for the average worker to easily commute to work and enjoy the benefits of a home with plenty of space. (Courtesy of Special Collections and Preservation Division, Chicago Public Library.)

the quality of urban life for all of Chicago's residents. She provided leadership for a civic movement that focused on the need to improve urban life, including education, social services, and urban housing. The planning and architecture of Chicago's new neighborhoods directly responded to Jane Addams' call to improve the quality of life for the city's residents.

Beginning in the early 1900s and continuing for nearly 40 years, Chicago's outer neighborhoods like Jefferson Park, Marquette Park, Austin, South Shore, and Beverly all grew with the promise of a new and healthy lifestyle. Developers and builders touted these new residential communities as well positioned between the "American Prairie" to the west and the "Great Metropolis" on Lake Michigan. A quote from a typical advertisement in April of 1919 states, "In the history of Chicago, there has never been offered to the people a more valuable opportunity than in Marquette Manor. What was a few years ago farm land, today has been developed into a high class residential subdivision, and no money was spared to accomplish this purpose and to make this property the finest home spot on the great Southwest Side." The "home spot" so often mentioned in advertisements was a single family home on its own parcel of land, also known as the Chicago Bungalow.

This Arts and Crafts-style bungalow was typical of California bungalows but was occasionally built in Chicago. While this bungalow on North Mozart clearly has design features that had more in common with homes in Pasadena, its brick construction reflected Chicago preferences. (Photograph by Mati Maldre.)

The Arts and Crafts style had a direct influence on the development of the Chicago Bungalow. That movement gained popularity in England in the mid-1800s, and migrated to America by the end of the century. As goods and products in England evolved from being produced by hand to being manufactured for mass production, many individuals, especially within the artistic and academic professions, argued against the homogeneity and lack of personalization that could result in an industrialized nation. They promoted the maintenance and strengthening of the special character and individuality of each person. Arts and Crafts practitioners focused on fusing work and art through the daily routines of the working class. They believed that this combination would lead to a higher quality of life.

Initially, Arts and Crafts ideas, promoting a home as a private retreat from bustling modern society, resulted in small vacation cottages on the East Coast as well as in larger and more elaborate houses on the West Coast. Most characteristic of Arts and Crafts houses, in both the east and west, was that they were made of wood and stucco construction with large open-air front porches. The architect, furniture maker, and editor, Gustav Stickley, promoted many of the Arts and Crafts ideals through his magazine, *The Craftsman*, published between 1901 and 1916.

Various magazines such as *House Beautiful, Better Homes and Gardens, The Ladies' Home Journal,* and *The Craftsman* touted Arts and Crafts principals. Simultaneously, architects in Chicago like Louis Sullivan and Frank Lloyd Wright developed a new definition of architectural style that broke free of historic European style, and better represented the ideals of America—new lands, new technologies, new citizens, and new ways of living. The "Prairie School" has most often been characterized as the unique Midwestern architectural achievement, often overshadowing the Chicago Bungalow. In reality, the Prairie School grew out of the Arts and Crafts Movement and had a profound effect on the development of the Chicago Bungalow, which combined the two earlier movements, creating affordable and stylish homes for Chicagoans leaving older industrial neighborhoods at the city's core.

Great variety in form and detail has been achieved in the appearance of the Chicago Bungalow by overlaying numerous architectural variations and Arts and Crafts ideals. Also, through the attention to issues pertinent to Chicago's social reform movements at the turn of the twentieth century, interior floor plans and amenities exhibit simple, functional, and sanitary attributes.

THE BUNGALOW CONTEXT

Following the philosophy of the Arts and Crafts Movement, Chicago Bungalows are situated on a single lot with a garden, in harmony with the environment. *Radford's Artistic Homes Catalogue*, published in Chicago in 1908, states, ". . . as to the location of the house, it should not be placed in the middle of the lot. To provide lawn room and a place for shrubbery and flower beds the house should be at one side or well back so that when the lawn decorations are placed, the picture will be artistic and the grounds will seem to be really a part of the house. Often this point is overlooked and an otherwise stylish house is

This bungalow appearing in the American Builder *shows the influence of the Prairie School with its emphasis on horizontal lines. The floor plan reflects the Arts and Crafts Movement's emphasis on an open and connected living space within. (*American Builder, *October 1919.)*

ruined by being out of harmony with the lot on which it sits."

During the mid-1800s, landscape architect Andrew Jackson Downing advocated placing the front of houses in garden-like settings and locating the kitchen and other secondary workspaces in back away from the main entrance. In Chicago, the romantic idea of a house on its own lot surrounded by landscaping had great appeal to urban city dwellers sharing apartments and flats. Today, mature trees in grass-covered parkways line Chicago Bungalow streets, providing a canopy of shade during the summer.

Victorian-era landscaping placed exotic plants in formal and rigid configurations to be viewed as "objects of art." Whereas natural gardens with irregular plantings of local origin better expressed the views of the Arts and Crafts doctrine, and as such, the Chicago Bungalow, which was built with inside rooms and outside landscaping blending together. Foundation plantings were the landscaping style of choice. Usually shrubs were planted close to the house, masking the seam between the wall and the ground. The most popular plants were evergreens, which required little maintenance and offered excellent screening and year-round color. Nurseries promoted them heavily and began mass-producing them specifically for this purpose. The typical design consisted of columned shrubs at either end of the house with spreading varieties underneath the windows between.

Views from the house focused toward natural gardens and window boxes with plantings that varied as the seasons changed. Flowers and lawns greeted each passerby, bringing a smile to friends and strangers alike. Each home and front lawn joined with the others to

This view of Christiana at Balmoral looking north in the winter of 1935 shows the extensive tree canopy on this mixed block of bungalows and other types of residences. (Courtesy of Special Collections and Preservation Division, Chicago Public Library.)

create a street that was pleasant, civil, and safe for parents and children to talk and play. Neighbors joined block clubs and communities were formed upon shared beliefs and common goals.

DEFINING ELEMENTS OF THE CHICAGO BUNGALOW

The Chicago Bungalow is a one-and-one-half-story single family home. It is rectangular in form consisting of solid brick construction with face brick and stone trim, topped with a low-pitched roof with wide overhangs. The building has generous windows, a full basement, and includes the modern amenities of central heat, electric service, and indoor plumbing. Most often, Chicago Bungalows are found side-by-side lining each side of the street, creating a neighborhood of similar yet distinct homes, where the entire view is as great as is the view of a single home. The similarity of homes helped neighbors build strong and unified communities. Many Chicago Bungalows were built from plans that were based on or modified from the catalogs of house plans that were being sold to builders.

The long, narrow city lots, usually 25 to 37 feet wide by 125 feet deep, helped shape Chicago Bungalows. The buildings stand side by side with other bungalows, separated by approximately 5 to 15 feet. The narrow front of the house directly faces the street. The building front is set back from the public sidewalk approximately 10 to 25 feet. Garages are located at the back of the lot, accessed through public service alleys dividing Chicago's residential blocks. Alleys in Chicago allowed for the absence of curb cuts along streets and

A row of houses along the 8300 block of South Halsted Street shows how similar these bungalows were in scale and mass. Detail differences, however, in dormers, limestone accents, brickwork, and windows are evident. For example, the house on the left has very narrow windowpanes that are not found in the other houses. (Photograph by Mati Maldre.)

sidewalks and provided a place for public garbage removal away from the fronts of the houses.

The Chicago street and alley land sub-division provided increased safety for residents by allowing neighbors to watch the activities on the street from front windows and porches. Front yard fences would rarely be installed, so that open and connected lawns could be shared and unite neighbors into a safe community. During earlier Victorian home building, it was typical for low fences to be installed around each home's property, clearly separating one house and property from the next.

The approach to a Chicago Bungalow from the sidewalk was accomplished with a narrow concrete walk located perpendicular to the street, either along the side of the front yard or gently curving up to the porch. The main entrance door most often stands under a small covered porch, four to five steps up from the sidewalk. The entrance and porch are located off-center on the front of the house or located along the sidewall to suggest an informal and friendly welcome. The Chicago Bungalow directly faces onto the sidewalk and street and is welcoming with gracious front windows and steps, individualized with special architectural

The front steps were the ideal place for children to connect with their neighbors under the watchful eye of family and friends. This photo shows the Beiriger and Clark children sitting on the steps of a bungalow at 7545 South Wentworth Avenue about 1938, while their uncle, John Beiriger, keeps an eye on them. (Courtesy of Gail Pelc.)

shapes and materials and self-contained with a large sheltering roof and eaves.

The front porch, covered by an overhanging roof, straddles between the inside and outside of the Chicago Bungalow. The porch can be used as an outside room to enjoy warm summer evenings and can also be used as an inside room for shelter from cold rainy days. A small covered porch, large enough to allow for a couple of chairs, provides an informal place to sit and watch over the neighborhood. The idea of a small outdoor room in the form of a porch provided a civil and healthy seat close to nature. A distinguishing characteristic of the Chicago Bungalow is the enclosure of the large open-air full front porch typically found in other bungalow house styles. The Chicago Bungalow retains a small open-air covered entrance and front porch. The remaining front porch area is enclosed in the shape of a rectangular or angled bay that is an extension of the living room.

Stepping brick walls topped with limestone and capped with large stone urns to connect the house with the surrounding yard and garden bordered the porch stairs. In some cases, a side entrance porch roof extended out and over a side driveway, though most automobiles entered a garage from the alley.

A particularly special characteristic of the Chicago Bungalow was its many windows to provide light, air, and a feeling of openness connecting to the gardens and landscaping outside. Chicago Bungalows have groups of windows on the exterior walls, especially the

Bungalow windows came in all shapes and sizes and designs but served the same purpose—they brought the outdoors inside. The strong vertical and horizontal lines in the windows blend to create a wall of light in this warm living room in the Gregory House, a bungalow bed and breakfast in Chicago's Andersonville neighborhood. (Photograph by Mati Maldre.)

The window placement on this corner home at 2834 West Marquette Road illustrates the emphasis on light and airiness. Windows open into each living space: the basement, dining room, and kitchen on the first floor, and the attic. While the windows for each space are different in size, they share the same vertical rhythm and create a pleasing unity. (Photograph by Mati Maldre.)

front wall, containing three to four double-hung windows in the living room and two or three roof dormer windows watching over the street. On the side of the house, two to three double-hung windows lined the dining room wall, with the kitchen, bedrooms, and bathroom having single windows. Housing reform advocates in the early 1900s highlighted the need to have sunlight and air reach every room in a house to be healthful.

In many cases, the Chicago Bungalow living room projects out from the front wall into the yard, as a full-story square or angled bay lined with windows. The upper sash of the living room windows will often be filled with decorative colored and cut glass patterns. As well, wooden-framed storm windows are hinged to protect the glass and to provide additional insulation for the rooms inside.

At the front and the back of the house, a small windowed dormer pokes up from the roof to provide light and air into the attic. Even panes of glass in the dormers and basements are sometimes filled with decorative patterns of leaded glass. Most often, the patterns and colors of decoration within the glass form geometric shapes echoing images of landscaping and nature.

To generate a great variety of designs and to provide each house with a unique appearance, builders used many sizes and shapes of windows. They often divided glass in the wood double-hung windows into intricate patterns. Small squares and rectangles or special cut and colored glass panels created diverse patterns. And even with such great variety, window-opening designs always aligned within a well-defined horizontal band, wrapping around the house to accentuate a simple and uncluttered appearance.

Local brick manufacturers flourished as developers constructed houses to keep up with population increases and housing demand. Because Chicago Bungalows were built with solid brick construction, not brick veneer over wood frame, they were fire protected, sturdy, and long lasting, with little maintenance, and were well insulated to maximize energy efficiency in Chicago's cold weather climate. A special brick known as "face brick" covered the front wall of the bungalow, whereas the side and back walls were of "standard" or "common brick." Face brick has a more decorative appearance than common brick. Builders often extended face brick back from the front, along the sidewalls approximately 10 feet to present a harmonious neighborhood appearance and located the lower priced and plainer common brick out of sight. Chicago Bungalows on corner parcels were often larger and more elaborate than those built side by side. Both the front and side of the house that faced the sidewalk and street were built with more expensive face brick and often had matching garages at the rear of the lot. The garages were built with face brick toward the street, matching roof materials and decorative stone insets identical to the house. The great variety of textures, colors, and combinations of face brick allowed for each house, though similar in overall shape, to be distinguished and individualized, thereby creating interesting and diverse rows of homes within blocks and neighborhoods.

Bands of limestone often bordered the face brick. Just above the level of the yard, a band of limestone separated face brick from the rough finish of the concrete basement foundation wall. The limestone band provided a finished base for various shapes and angles of brick walls to be built beneath the rows of windows. A band of limestone also topped the brick wall and again provided a base for rows of windows. Additionally, a third limestone band would top the windows to support the brick up to the underside of the roof overhang.

The overall effect of the bands of limestone, separating the concrete foundation, brick walls, rows of windows, and roof eave, give the Chicago Bungalow a very solid, horizontal, earth-hugging appearance. In addition, horizontal decorative brick patterns, limestone insets, and window boxes are accented by vertical window framing and "earth to roof" brick piers and pilasters and reinforce the building's sturdy rectangular geometry.

Limestone insets are often used in Chicago Bungalows. From intricate and complicated decorative wall stone to windowsills, stair and pier caps, special masonry appointments differentiate each bungalow from its neighbor. The light color of the limestone would often contrast with the darker brick colors, thereby highlighting and accenting the decorative and horizontal character of the house, and providing a smaller and friendlier scale to the building. Common to almost every Chicago Bungalow are stone window box brackets built into the front wall under the living room windows. On these brackets sat stone window boxes, all built for the new homeowner's enjoyment of nature. Even in some cases, cut limestone spouts were installed as part of the porch wall to drain rainwater

Corner houses were usually the most expensive homes on the block as they had a prominent position and required greater expense in detailing and more expensive materials. This corner house in the suburb of Berwyn has face brick along both street fronts and creates an attractive and formidable point of entry to the block. (Photograph by Mati Maldre.)

The choice of face brick colors and textures was one means by which a builder created a personality for the bungalow. As face brick was more expensive to make, it was reserved for the front of bungalows, and common brick was used on the sides and backs of most homes.

*Common brick was produced in Chicago, but manufacturers outside of Chicago with access to better quality clay supplied face brick. (*American Builder, *May 1923.)*

Why It Pays to Use Face Brick!

Structural Reasons –

1 Size and Form Please the Eye
2 Adapts to Mason's Skill
3 Strength Far Beyond Needs
4 Never Rots nor Fades
5 Strictly Fireproof

A·F·B·A
USE FACE BRICK
—it Pays

"By Frost, nor Fire, nor Flood, nor Even Time are Well-Burned Clays Destroyed"

USE FACE BRICK–*it Pays*

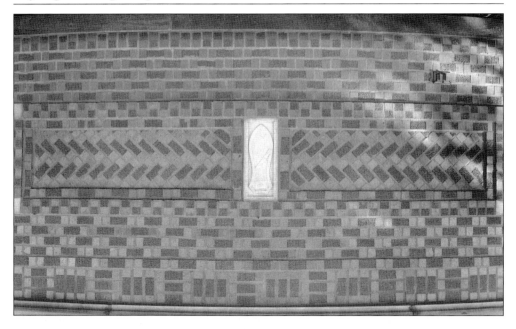

In this detail of a bungalow front at 9640 South Hamilton, face brick and limestone accents combine to create a signature for the homeowner. There are at least four kinds of face brick and four patterns of brick surrounding the distinctive herringbone pattern at the center. (Photograph by Mati Maldre.)

This American Builder *feature explained the best way to lay courses of common brick. In 1924, the Illinois Brick Company, Chicago's largest brick manufacturer, produced more than 700 million common bricks for the building boom then underway. (*American Builder, *January 1921.)*

The brickwork of a bungalow chimney at 6634 South Whipple shows the effect of striking the mortar joints. By striking, masons accented the space between the bricks as well as making each brick take on its own identity. The step work and the soldier course of brickwork and limestone create a unique identity for this bungalow. (Photograph by Mati Maldre.)

onto the surrounding plantings. In a few instances, terra cotta insets were used to accent the brick walls and to add special character to the Chicago Bungalow.

The patterns of the brick often created a variety of shadows on the front of the house to increase its uniqueness. Some of these brick patterns were achieved by laying the bricks in certain directions and various locations. For example, setting the bricks on end, next to each other, creates what is known as a "Soldier Course," or placing the ends of bricks side by side every fifth or sixth layer, is known as an "American Bond."

Even the color of the mortar between the bricks was carefully considered to support the visual interest of the house. A mortar color that would contrast with the brick emphasized the individual bricks in the wall, whereas mortar that was similar in color to the brick provided an appearance of being monolithic and solid.

The low-pitched, hip styled roof covering a Chicago Bungalow is a dominant feature of the house. The large overhanging roof is both a visual symbol sheltering and functionally protecting the house from the outside. The simple shape of the roof over the main house is punctuated with small dormers centered over the front and back walls. Dormers are roofed in a variety of shapes, though most common is a hip, gable, or combination.

The most common roofing material for Chicago bungalows was asphalt shingle. In more expensive homes, builders used slate and tile roofing for its endurance and attractive colors. This detail of a tile roof shows the elegance and beauty that tile contributes to the home at 66th and Troy. (Photograph by Mati Maldre.)

Generally, the roof is covered with asphalt shingles and in some cases with clay tiles. The base of the roof is accented with a wide horizontal fascia and large eaves overhanging the outside walls. Below the overhanging fascia, decorative limestone, or wood trim symbolically support the roof above.

INTERIOR BUNGALOW ELEMENTS

In an effort to make the house affordable for first-time buyers, Chicago Bungalows were built with similar floor plans, allowing the variety and diversity of the houses to be expressed with different materials and colors on the building fronts. Typical floor plans usually included six rooms on the first floor (living, dining, kitchen, bath, and two bedrooms), an unfinished attic and basement, as well as a front porch and rear steps.

The Chicago Bungalow provided many of the amenities of earlier "Victorian" mansions, albeit scaled down in size. For example, a covered porch, entrance vestibule, and separate dining room, as well as an attic and basement were all found in earlier homes of the wealthy. Gardens, flower boxes, and planters were all drawn from the landscape of the private country estates. Developers provided central heat, built-in furniture, leaded decorative glass, fireplaces, carved stone, fancy brickwork, plaster walls, an abundance of hardwood floors, doors and trim, and solid brick construction in these new freestanding homes for the first-time home buyer.

The interior materials and colors of the Chicago Bungalow were in keeping with the notion of having a new, simple, and sanitary lifestyle in harmony with nature. Carpenters installed hardwood floors and doors. They left these unpainted and instead varnished to present the quality and beauty of the natural wood. Plaster and lathe walls provided solid separation and substantial sound reduction between rooms. Owners often decorated or accented these with horizontal sections of wallpaper or stenciling, relating to the horizontal limestone and brick bands on the outside of the house. Often, the paint colors for the walls and wall coverings followed the colors of nature.

The front entry door was built to be gracious and welcoming. Cut limestone framed the door opening separating the brick wall from the wood frame of the door. The varnished entry door comprised of solid oak panels had a window opening to see visitors. Sometimes decorative art glass mixed between the clear glass panels of the door window. Patterns of nature often ornamented brass door handles, doorknockers, and mail slots. The overall effect of the frame, door, windows, and hardware was one of an artistic assemblage of small

*Kitchen floors were most often maple and all other rooms were of oak. The development of specialized machinery made possible the production of large quantities of high quality flooring at affordable prices. (*American Builder, *May 1923.)*

25

pieces creating a unique and thoughtful passageway into the house. Beyond the porch, the front door opened into an intimate interior vestibule. An art glass window positioned next to the front door most often washed the vestibule with colored light. A small coat closet providing storage for coats, boots, and umbrellas also opened into the interior vestibule.

Within a couple of steps, the view focuses into the adjoining living room and dining room. The living room is the central room of the house, where the family would gather and socialize. The other rooms in the house supported the daily activities of the living room. This change of emphasis from earlier and more formal houses with a central kitchen and guest parlor highlight the changing form of family interaction during the early 1900s.

On the far wall of the living room, a small fireplace faces the entry vestibule. The fireplace is centered on the wall, often between built-in wooden bookcases with decorative glass windows above. Even though the functional need for a fireplace had diminished with new central heating, the fireplace was built as a luxurious focus of shared pleasure for the family. Ceramic art tile depicting scenes and colors of nature sometimes surrounded the fireplace hearth.

The most important room in the house was the living room, and central to the living room was the fireplace as can be seen in this photograph of the Gregory House. Typically located in the center of the wall, farthest from the point of entry, the fireplace beckoned family and guests to gather around. In more modest homes, fireplaces often used gas and eliminated the need to construct a chimney. (Photograph by Mati Maldre.)

Through an arched opening, without interruption of doors or closed hallways, the living room connected to the dining room. Usually, large enough for a table of six to eight people, the dining room table is where the family meals were served. Along the wall between the kitchen and dining room, a built-in china cabinet provided storage for dinnerware and family needs. A small hallway off the dining room provided access to one bedroom at either end of the hall, as well as shielded the entrance into a bathroom. Bedrooms and bathrooms were arranged so that each room could be privately entered off the hallway and not directly from another room. Earlier working-class cottages and middle-class apartments were often built with bedrooms entering directly off the kitchen, dining, and living rooms.

The bathroom included a toilet, sink, and bathtub, all with modern operating plumbing. Additionally, the bathroom came with a small built-in closet and a medicine cabinet with a mirror. Easy to clean furnishings and durable room materials dominated the bathroom design. Decorative light colored ceramic tile covered floors and walls. Standard interior furnishings included white ceramic pedestal sinks and built-in bathtubs.

Architects located the front bedroom between the living room, the bathroom, and the second bedroom that adjoined the back wall of the bathroom. In three-bedroom homes, a third bedroom stood at the rear house wall. Bedrooms were provided with built-in clothes closets, and a small closet in the hall provided room for linens. As well, a laundry slot to the

In this Andersonville bungalow, living spaces flow together naturally. The large entry way replaced the narrow passages common to nineteenth-century homes and connected the living and dining rooms. (Photograph by Mati Maldre.)

Bathrooms were small and efficient and employed nonporous materials such as ceramic tile, porcelain, and enamel-coated cast iron. Chicago's Chas. F. Lorenzen & Co. claimed to be "America's Largest Tile Jobbers." This advertisement calls the ideal bathroom one with "snow white tile covering." (American Builder, *April 1922.*)

basement was often built into the wall of the hallway next to the bedrooms. Electric outlets and fixtures provided convenient lighting and energy in all the rooms of a Chicago Bungalow.

Residents entered the kitchen just off of the dining room, next to a stair door that led to the attic. Builders constructed bungalow kitchens compactly with modern conveniences, including a sink with plumbing, an icebox or later a refrigerator, and a gas or electric stove. Generally bungalows contained small kitchens designed solely for the preparation of food. Laundry and additional chores were to be done in other parts of the home. Bungalow dwellers ate meals in the dining room or in cozy breakfast nooks provided in many plans. Built-in slots in the rear wall of the house allowed the direct delivery of ice to the bottom of the built-in icebox. Cabinets and even built-in ironing boards were often found in kitchens. Often, because of the small kitchen, builders included small linear "Pullman"-style kitchen units in the house. A "Pullman"-style kitchen featured cabinets, a sink, counter, and stove all assembled into a single line along one wall of the kitchen. Simplicity and cleanliness dominated the design of the kitchen as it had the entire bungalow. A rear door off the kitchen opened outside to a small, uncovered, wooden porch with steps down to the back yard. The back yard was approximately 40 feet long to the wall of the garage and 25 to 37 feet wide.

One of the Most Popular Innovations in Building Constru on During the Last Few Years is the Outdoor Icing Regrigerat Saves the Housewife Considerable Labor.

*Many bungalows had special doors built into the rear wall so that the iceman could make his delivery directly into the icebox from the back porch. This illustration shows the arrangement of the special door and the icebox. (*American Builder, c. 1921.)

The home in the foreground looks the way the rest of the bungalows in the 2500 block of 61st Avenue in Cicero appeared when built. Over time, homeowners enclosed their porches to create additional living spaces. (Photograph by Mati Maldre.)

Off the kitchen, a narrow stair led to the attic. Builders left the attic unfinished to provide for future expansion at a later date. Because the builder saved money by not having to finish the attic, home buyers benefited with lower home prices. The attic included adequate height to allow some floor area to be used, up to the slope of the roof. At each end of the roof, a dormer allowed space for additional headroom, as well as for light and air through small double-hung windows. Occasionally a side dormer provided additional useable floor area with higher ceilings, as well as extra windows. A brick chimney passed through the attic, from the basement to above the roof.

Another staircase led to the unfinished full-length basement. Well-placed windows dispersed light around the perimeter of the large undivided room. Here below the first floor raised about 4 feet above the outside ground level, architects provided space for laundry facilities and heating plants. The open floor plan of a Chicago Bungalow resulted in part from the new central heating systems. The basement provided convenient space to locate this central heating system. A hot water or steam boiler, fueled by coal, oil, or gas, connected to radiators in each room of the house. Also, a rear door into and out of the basement allowed for delivery and easy access to storage and the boiler.

Chicago Bungalows are beautiful structures—warm, utilitarian, and personable. They endure today due to their thoughtful design, use of high quality materials and craftsmanship, and to their civic neighborliness. Chicago Bungalows stand as a testament that fine architecture is not a function of unlimited dollars but of good design.

two

BUNGALOWS AND THE COMPLEX ORIGIN OF THE MODERN HOUSE

by Joseph Biggott

This working-class cottage on Chicago's North Side included a large front porch and a typical floor plan that provided a model for the future development of the Chicago Bungalow. (Courtesy of Special Collections, Sulzer Regional Library, Chicago Public Library.)

When architectural historians first considered Chicago's built environment, they focused upon the city's most notable structures, the skyscrapers. Two generations later, intellectuals continue to praise the distinctive qualities of Chicago's first tall buildings. Most often, they have employed historical arguments to justify the type of modern building they consider aesthetically pleasing.

In contrast, few critics have found satisfaction in the common residential structures that dominate metropolitan Chicago. Many regard these buildings as an aesthetic blight, the unfortunate consequence of suburban sprawl. So despite their ubiquity, common urban house forms have not received the historical attention given the handful of exceptional buildings that serve as monuments downtown. Consequently, we know very little about the origins of the common structures that served as the location for everyday life in Chicago and most other industrial cities.

Historians have neglected structures such as the bungalow, because they derive from processes with less aesthetic appeal than those that produced the skyscraper. The first section of this essay will argue that a majority of Chicago's bungalows evolved from common working-class house forms and construction practices developed in the nineteenth century. At that time, the city was attracting large numbers of immigrants, who created a huge demand for working-class residences. By the turn of the century, a few simple forms accommodated a wide range of circumstances, allowing new construction to provide housing for even the poorest groups within the city.

During the next generation, the housing market shifted in two directions to meet the demands created by an increasingly diverse working-class population. First, it responded to the arrival of large numbers of impoverished southern and eastern Europeans. To house these immigrants, Chicago developed crowded, inner city neighborhoods of the type made famous by reformers such as Jane Addams. However, during the high tide of immigration, the market also accommodated a more secure population that included second- and third-generation Chicagoans. This more prosperous segment of the working class became the primary beneficiaries of new residential construction during the 1920s. After this date, the market seldom built new houses for poorer members of the working class. Instead, bungalows accommodated a greatly expanded range within the middle ranks of society. The change in the market led to a slow transformation as class-based neighborhoods became more common than neighborhoods based upon ethnic and religious heritage.

Of course, like the more dramatic skyscraper, the bungalow was not unique to Chicago. The product of an increasingly industrial economy, Chicago's bungalows contained the same millwork, plumbing, heating, and electrical components as houses built in other places. Indeed, after 1910, many common houses in Chicago resembled others built throughout the United States. Historians have attributed these developments to an evolving middle-class culture whose comforts and privileges trickled down to the less advantaged as large manufacturers adopted methods of "mass" production. But the development of a wide range of stylish common houses was not so simple a process.

The second and third sections of this essay describe the more stylish bungalow as a complex product whose components required both flexible and standardized systems of manufacture. To a degree, these modifications resulted from modest but steady

This 1909 view of the Chicago Lawn community shows Victorian homes clustered near 63rd Street and the large expanse of land waiting for development. Most of these empty lots would be built up with bungalows in the 1920s. (Courtesy of Chicago Lawn Historical Society.)

improvements in the common, working-class houses that had been the standard form for Chicago builders since the 1880s. However, the housing boom of the 1920s altered construction practices throughout the United States by creating a tremendous demand for common houses with modern conveniences. The boom generated the volume necessary for investments in production facilities that allowed manufacturers to produce a wider range of fashionable decorative elements, as well as the more utilitarian plumbing, heating, and electrical components that distinguished the modern house.

In Chicago, developers most often identified this new form of housing as a "bungalow." Standard forms included a range of components supplied by a diverse group of manufacturers who employed various production methods to satisfy consumer demands. To supply fashionable, and often expensive, components, the woodworking industry retained older, flexible methods of production that provided house buyers with a wide range of options. In contrast, large plumbing firms such as Crane, Kohler, and American Sanitary adopted capital intensive methods of production to supply a greater volume of modestly priced, standardized fixtures. By doing so, plumbing suppliers limited consumer choice so that even the most distinctive bungalows had utilitarian fixtures that were nearly identical to those found in houses throughout the Midwest. Never a simple product of "mass" production, the bungalow required a complex variety of components that allowed Chicago's builders to adapt local forms to meet the needs of an expanding and increasingly diverse middle class.

THE EVOLUTION OF COMMON FORMS

During the building boom of the 1880s, Chicagoans accepted a dominant form of urban house that served as the building block for neighborhoods throughout the metropolitan region. The form was called a workingman's cottage. The simplest cottages were one-story, frame, rectangular structures of four, five, or six rooms. The bedrooms were located on one side of the house, the parlor, dining room, and kitchen on the other. Simple cottages were plain and unadorned. However, the form could be expanded and improved easily to meet the needs of a diverse population. In many instances, builders added porches, basements, and various forms of architectural embellishment, which made the cottage a substantial house.

The number of cottages expanded significantly during the 1880s, as a result of the real estate boom that accompanied industrial expansion in outlying areas of the city. To meet the needs of a predominantly working-class population, local real estate syndicates marketed inexpensive properties aggressively, claiming that home ownership was a reward within reach of any honest workman. While large developers occasionally built rows of simple cottages, one after another, most neighborhoods contained a variety of houses built by many different carpenters. Within these neighborhoods, simple forms were modified in two ways. First, cottages were built with two stories to serve as apartments or commercial buildings. The common commercial building in Chicago had a business on the first floor and living space above. Typical apartments were the equivalent of two cottages, one placed on top of the other. These structures provided their owners with additional income from rent. Before 1940, Chicago's two-story apartments and commercial buildings were as likely to be owned by an occupant as single-family residences.

Second, larger and more elaborate cottages were built for prosperous members of the working class. The most expensive cottages had a formal front hall with a staircase to the second story. Prior to the introduction of bathrooms, formal hallways were the most costly features of a simple house. They required an elaborate staircase. One-and-one-half and two-story, single-family cottages had a major advantage over a one-story residence. They allowed some bedrooms to be located upstairs on a level separate from the parlor, dining room, and kitchen. Many owners desired the separation but did not wish to pay for a formal hallway. In these instances, builders placed a less elaborate stairway in the parlor or constructed an unadorned stairway in the center of the house. During the nineteenth century, a formal hall served an important function in an emerging middle-class culture. Formal halls allowed middle-class families to practice an elaborate etiquette when entertaining guests. In contrast, when someone walked through the front door of a working-class house, they entered the parlor directly.

For decades, historians have dismissed cottages as inferior housing. They have based their condemnations on the evidence presented by Progressive reformers, most notably Edith Abbott. Abbott's history of Chicago's tenement problem described cottages as the universally substandard product of an unregulated market for housing. During the 1930s, she favored federal involvement in programs that would allow experts to design superior residences for the poor. Most historians have accepted Abbott's work at face value. In doing so, they have failed to recognize the diverse conditions created by the market for working-class cottages.

Obviously, during the high tide of immigration from southern and eastern Europe, many cottages became dilapidated and obsolete just as the reformers suggested. In crowded neighborhoods throughout the city and its industrial suburbs, single-family cottages were raised on brick foundations, converting the original structure into a multiple-family building. In the worst cases, obsolete cottages were moved to the rear of a lot so the owner could build a much larger brick tenement on the front of the lot. Abbott regarded dilapidated rear houses without plumbing and adequate heating as one of the great social evils in Chicago. Their proliferation led to neighborhoods that crowded building upon building, leaving no space for back yards and gardens.

Historians must acknowledge the severe social problems that resulted from poverty and rapid urbanization at the beginning of the century. However, their concerns for the failures of the housing market should not lead them to dismiss the many instances when it was successful. A large number of cottages were decent one- and two-family houses that were improved and updated with time. Throughout Chicago, owners enlarged small cottages and added plumbing and electricity. These transformations occurred in neighborhoods that housed southern and eastern Europeans, as well as in areas that housed more prosperous groups among the working class.

The gradual acquisition of improvements was critical to the development of a modern housing market. Without such a process, most families could not have purchased a house. Initially, the installation of plumbing, electricity, and sewer connections were prohibitively expensive, especially for the great numbers of poor, young families with children. Consequently, thousands of recently arrived families purchased very small houses with the intention of adding amenities piecemeal, when they could afford them. The immigrant poor in Detroit, Cleveland, Milwaukee, and Toledo followed similar strategies, producing very high levels of home ownership. While inefficient and wasteful, the process worked for many. Ignored in the accounts of housing reformers, it produced a general improvement in the quality of common houses, especially in newer sections of the city and suburbs.

In 1910, metropolitan Chicago contained tens of thousands of inexpensive modern houses, owned by families from even the poorest groups in the city. By this time, most new cottages were built with plumbing and electrical service and five or six rooms. Even the addition of one room in a common house affected family life significantly. The typical five-room house had two bedrooms, one for parents and the other for children. In a six-room house, the additional bedroom allowed a family to create separate sleeping spaces for boys and girls. Large families especially preferred houses with a greater number of rooms. Often, they compromised on the size of rooms in the house, creating very small rooms to allow space for an additional bedroom.

In outlying portions of the city, where lots were larger and less crowded, modern cottages had space for back yards with trees and gardens. Throughout Chicago, neighborhoods still testify to the effects of modernization on cottage housing. The shift became more pronounced during the 1920s, when the city experienced another major boom in residential construction. Once again, local developers engaged in aggressive

This winter scene of a bungalow backyard on Dakin Street shows the various fruit trees planted by the owner. Backyards became favorite places to grow fruits, vegetables, and flowers. (Courtesy of Anonymous Donor.)

campaigns aimed at a very large segment of the population. During this boom, advertisements called the most popular new houses "bungalows" rather than "cottages."

Distinctions between improved, modern cottages and modest, one-story bungalows were minor. The floor plans were identical: parlor, dining room, and kitchen on one side of the house, bedrooms on the other. Both had plumbing, electrical and gas service, and often central heating. The most significant difference was the structure of the roof. Bungalows replaced the steep front gable of the cottage with a less pitched roof that had a hip rafter facing the street. In addition, a majority of bungalows built within the city limits of Chicago were brick. The type often recognized as the "classic" Chicago Bungalow altered slightly the floor plan of the traditional cottage. Cottages often had an attached porch that ran the entire length of the front of the house. The classic bungalow expanded the parlor or created a sunroom in a manner that increased the interior space of the house and reduced the size and prominence of the front porch.

The bungalow style affected apartment construction as well as single-family housing. The new apartment form was called a "two-flat." Usually, it was a brick structure with a flat roof that, like earlier apartments, stacked one single-family floor plan on top of another. The flat roof gave the two-flat a different appearance from the low-lying, classic Chicago Bungalow. However, in Cicero, Berwyn, and a few other locations, single-family bungalows were sometimes built with flat roofs. In many cases, two-flats were built in long rows, on blocks without single-family bungalows. This practice segregated single-family and multiple-family houses within a neighborhood. In large developments, realtors placed special emphasis on corner lots. Whether two-flats or bungalows, these residences were the most elaborate on a given block. Corner houses had decorative face brick on at least two sides of the structure. On the interior of the block, common bungalows used more expensive materials only on the narrow portion of the house that faced the street.

In these instances, bungalows evolved incrementally from Chicago's dominant local house form of the nineteenth century. Variants of the cottage and bungalow forms reappeared again in working-class areas of metropolitan Chicago during the building booms of the 1950s and 1960s. Over the course of three generations, these structures testified to the tenacity of vernacular traditions that can produce variety within a familiar form. Certainly, these structures had no connection, other than linguistic, to the buildings in India that gave the bungalow its name.

However, in Chicago and other cities in the United States, bungalow designs were more than just a product of vernacular traditions evolving over time. After 1910, the city's common houses also derived from a national movement to make modern houses more stylish. At the highest end of the market, Chicagoans built bungalows influenced by the

This row of Marquette Park two-flats on the 6900 block of South Washtenaw shows bungalow style details while providing income property for owners, making home ownership easier for many who moved to the Bungalow Belt. (Photograph by Mati Maldre.)

These flat-roofed bungalows on 58th Court in Cicero exhibit a local variation on the bungalow theme. (Photograph by Mati Maldre.)

Arts and Crafts Movement. On the Northwest Side, on Avers, Hamlin, Harding, and Springfield Streets, the district known as "The Villa" contains many fine examples of such structures. Before the '20s, common builders also popularized this movement in a manner that affected modestly priced residences. Sometimes, the differences were cosmetic. Builders often varied the exterior of houses within a neighborhood by altering the roof of a one-story bungalow. They built less steeply pitched roofs, with gables on the side rather than the front of the house. Most of these houses maintained the traditional floor plan of the earlier cottage form, with bedrooms on one side of the house, parlor, dining room, and kitchen on the other.

Bungalows of one-and-one-half stories often had different floor plans. Many of these structures resembled the most expensive forms of cottages, with formal or informal stairways leading to second-floor bedrooms. However, some plans eliminated the linear arrangement of Chicago's traditional houses. The parlor, dining room, and kitchen no longer formed a straight line. Influenced by national trends, these houses had larger parlors, dining rooms, and kitchens arranged in a circular manner on the first floor, with bedrooms located on the second floor. One-and-one-half-story bungalows were usually at least 26 feet wide. Consequently, they required a lot with a frontage wider than the 25-

foot lots that accommodated narrow, rectangular cottages. During the 1920s, most new developments in metropolitan Chicago had lots with frontages of at least 30 feet. In outlying areas, lots with even larger frontages accommodated the new type of bungalow as well as a driveway for the family car.

The real estate boom of the 1920s affected an enormous portion of the metropolitan landscape. The housing created during the boom incorporated 40 years of adaptations in common house forms. Because of these advances, Chicagoans enjoyed many options when they considered the purchase of a modern house. The market included neighborhoods of modern cottages with plumbing and central heating. The older form appeared less desirable than the bungalow, which offered a greater variety of stylish components. Bungalow neighborhoods also offered wider lots that provided more space for gardens, trees, or garages. By the end of the boom, Chicago had established a complex metropolitan market for real estate, with clear distinctions between older, inner city neighborhoods and the Bungalow Belts that surrounded them.

Persons familiar with only portions of metropolitan Chicago can fail to appreciate the variety achieved within the Bungalow Belt. Within a given neighborhood, bungalows and two-flats usually were of similar design and cost. The Northwest Side, Beverly, and suburbs such as Cicero and Berwyn have distinctive rows of classic Chicago Bungalows and two-flats. However, the South Side, the Southern suburbs, Elmhurst, and Brookfield

This 1920s view of 72nd and Exchange Avenue in South Shore shows the construction of a bungalow. Notice the steam shovel on the next lot digging a foundation. (Courtesy of Special Collections and Preservation Division, Chicago Public Library.)

contain large numbers of frame bungalows that varied considerably in style and cost. Sometimes frame construction provided a cheaper alternative for those who could not afford a brick house. In other instances, frame bungalows were as costly as brick. These residences provided homeowners with a larger and more elaborate house for the same money as a smaller but sturdier brick house.

For residents of ethnic communities, the purchase of a bungalow, whether frame or brick, presented a significant choice. There were few bungalows in portions of the city that had been developed fully before 1920. These neighborhoods included the initial settlements of most southern and eastern European immigrants. So they contained the religious, cultural, and commercial institutions familiar to the first generations. Attracted by fashionable housing on the periphery, the more prosperous members of ethnic communities ventured to new sections of the city that mixed people of various nationalities. But the desire for new housing did not compel Chicagoans to forsake their pasts. Groups, especially Roman Catholics, established bungalow neighborhoods with religious institutions as their centerpiece. Even if they had gained only a small measure of security, families could abandon or reestablish traditional ways of life. Consequently, with improvements in the cottage and bungalow, Chicagoans fulfilled their social and cultural needs by expanding their options within the housing market. To meet these needs, the manufacturers of building components had to adopt methods of manufacture that met in various ways the demands of fashion and utility.

Czech Americans were among the first Central European ethnic groups to move in large numbers to the suburbs. By the 1920s, both Berwyn and Cicero contained large Czech-American populations. Pictured here is Vlasta (Svoboda) Shaw dressed in a Czech folk dress in her father's Berwyn backyard in the mid-1920s. (Courtesy of Barbara Hrbek.)

STANDARDIZATION AND THE FASHIONABLE MARKET: MILLWORK

In the 1830s, Chicago's early settlers established saw and planning mills soon after their arrival. The mills provided carpenters with the dimensional lumber, sills, lath, siding, sheathing, and flooring that were basic components for every house. Prior to 1880, the basic materials produced by mills required fitting on site. Individual pieces of dimensional lumber varied considerably in size. One "2-by-8" might measure 2-by-7-and-_ inches and another 2-by-8-and-_ inches. Because of irregularities, carpenters had to notch each of the floor joists prior to erecting a house frame in order to adjust for differences in size. Given such wide tolerances in so basic a component, it is not surprising that for the first 50 years of Chicago's history, carpenters used hand tools to make the doors, windows, and trim for the houses they built.

During the building boom of the 1880s, local carpenters could no longer supply the demand for the components of common houses. So local entrepreneurs invested in factories capable of producing standard features such as windows, doors, and trim. However, even the largest manufacturers of millwork did not pursue methods of "mass production." Substantial investments in systems for producing and assembling vast quantities of standardized parts could lead to financial ruin. Chicago's housing market always had been governed by cycles of boom and bust. Special purpose machines were expensive, and new systems of manufacture required considerable periods of trial and error. Consequently, the largest firms adopted flexible methods that allowed them to adjust to the whims of the market. They limited their purchases of special purpose machines and simply hired more workers during busy seasons when they struggled to meet the demand for millwork. Seasonal workers could be let go at the end of the building season, whereas machines represented more permanent and costly investments.

When woodworking firms mechanized, they did not do so to produce elaborate goods or reduce the costs of building components. They invested in new systems to meet the demand for standard products created by a rapidly expanding market for common houses. Certainly, factories supplied a more finished and polished product than the work produced by moderately skilled local carpenters. But the elaborate goods that produced the intricacies of a Queen Anne or a Victorian style remained labor-intensive, custom work. No matter how modern the factory, intricate work required hand labor by skilled workmen. Mechanization was restricted to the simple tasks of creating stock parts for standard goods. In a volatile market, manufacturers desired flexibility. They created plants that produced both extended runs of common goods, as well as batches of smaller but more expensive special orders.

During the past two decades, publishers have reprinted for a popular audience late-nineteenth and early-twentieth-century catalogs of various manufacturers of building components. These catalogs can deceive persons who do not consider carefully the nature of markets and manufacturing. Most catalogs advertised a cornucopia of elaborate merchandise, the full range of products offered by wholesalers for a market that ranged from the wealthy to the poor. However, a large millwork firm, such as Chicago's E.L. Roberts & Company, had less need to advertise stock items than elaborate goods.

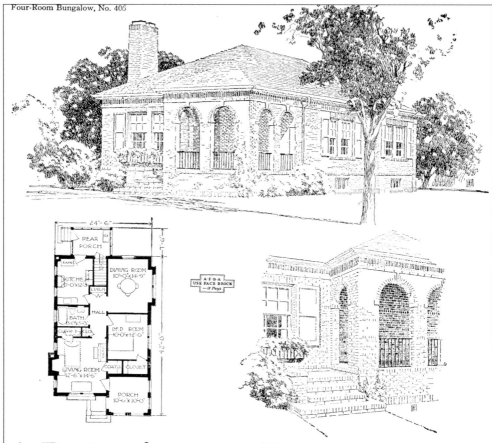

Four-Room Bungalow, No. 406

A Design from our "Bungalow Books"

THIS home, skillfully designed in a renaissance style, is one of our series of "Face Brick Bungalow and Small House Plans."

Its artistic handling and thoughtful interior arrangement are representative of the high architectural character of the 128 homes, designed by talented and experienced architects, which are presented in our four booklets.

Complete working drawings and masonry bills of material for all the designs given in these booklets

can be purchased for from $12 to $21, according to the number of rooms. These plans are for homes of from three to eight rooms.

The four booklets of "Face Brick Bungalow and Small House Plans" give you access to a remarkable collection of plans at a trifling cost. You will find frequent and effective use for them, and accordingly should secure a set at once. We will send them to you postpaid for $1, or single copies for 25¢. Address Department A. 10.

Every builder and contractor should have our other books: "The Story of Brick," which will be sent free; "The Home of Beauty," a book of delightful home designs submitted in architectural competition, price 50¢; and the "Manual of Face Brick Construction," an authentic text book of brick construction for the builder or layman, supplemented with thirty house designs in full colors, price $1. If you do not have these books, write for them now.

THE AMERICAN FACE BRICK ASSOCIATION
110 South Dearborn Street, Chicago

The Chicago-based American Face Brick Association offered a series of four booklets titled Face Brick Bungalow and Small House Plans *in 1921. The series included plans for 128 homes. Each booklet cost 25¢. Complete drawings ranged in price from $12–21. (*American Builder, *October 1921.)*

Windows, doors, and moldings were the staples of the industry, familiar to everyone in the building trades. In 1903, Robert's catalogue displayed 52 pages of standard moldings and their prices. The catalogue depicted these items simply, with only outlines of the shapes used to create standard trim for windows, doors, and other common features of the house. The company also guaranteed that the "moldings are smoothly manufactured and are strictly up to grade." In contrast, the catalog featured elaborate drawings and expensive photographs of its stair designs for parlors and halls. These designs involved special orders that required aggressive advertising. However, their prominence in the catalog did not mean that elaborate goods dominated the market or were the force behind advances in manufacture. Stock items provided the largest firms with the greatest volume of business.

After 1905, the introduction of variable speed electric motors, ball bearings, better quality tool steel, as well as larger manufacturing facilities increased the production and improved the quality of millwork. But the industry never achieved the technological precision that became common in metalworking, where the nature of steel as a material allowed for precision cutting and forming. Certainly, millwork firms never established mass production with assembly lines. In the most modern mills, workers continued to use hand trucks to move stacks of parts throughout factories, while common, relatively simple, repetitive tasks such as glazing windows continued to be labor-intensive activities that defied mechanization. As a result, standardization remained incomplete. Even after the bungalow boom of the '20s, the sizes for standard components of windows differed depending on the region of the country. In New York City, the rails and stiles of common windows were narrower than in Chicago, while in Cleveland and Pittsburgh they were longer.

Despite their limitations, modestly sized, flexible firms produced a wide range of standard products critical to the appearance of small houses. In 1923, H. Vandervoort Walsh of the School of Architecture at Columbia University argued that, more than any other feature, millwork either made or marred the appearance of structures such as the bungalow. Yet, when selecting millwork, the builder faced "the limitation of cost more exactingly imposed" than in any other feature of a house. Economy demanded the choice of stock materials of the plainest type. Nevertheless, bungalows became "artistic" because builders created variety by combining simply designed products in multiple ways. Walsh suggested that built-in furniture was worth the additional cost. He advised builders to consider carefully the value of built-in bookcases, window seats, mantels, china closets, breakfast benches, dressing tables, and radiator enclosures because they all added substantial and attractive qualities to the small house.

Popularly produced catalogs demonstrate that manufacturers achieved a variety of options for modest houses, despite the limitations imposed by the necessity for plain designs. By 1910, Sears sold nearly all of the components for constructing a house, including lumber, millwork, lighting fixtures, tile, furnaces, plumbing, and hardware. But Sears limited designs for its millwork. In 1910, it offered customers only five models of starting newel posts and two types of corner newels for the stairways sold in its catalogue. The company also advised against custom orders. Instead, it offered three standard designs and suggested that a competent local carpenter could assemble the appropriate one on site. A firm, such as E.L. Roberts, retained the ability to do specialty work, including custom stair building, because the firm did contract work for major hotels, banks, and restaurants. Sears never competed for these jobs, concentrating only on residential sales. By limiting its range of interests, the company promised lower costs and the ability to ship orders immediately, thereby avoiding the delay of two to three months common among firms producing custom-built stairs.

By 1926, Sears sold complete sets of construction materials for more than 70 houses, 29 of which the firm identified as bungalows. The houses offered a variety of options within a similar price range. For $2,124, the Hamilton was a one-story, five-room frame bungalow with a classic Chicago floor plan. It included a fireplace, built-in bench, and a breakfast alcove. For $2,076, the Vallonia was a larger but plainer structure. It was a one-and-one-half-story bungalow with an attic that, when finished for an additional $247, provided space for three very small bedrooms. In both cases, the illustrations of the interiors suggest simplicity in design. They also show the significance of new furniture styles in creating distinctive bungalows. Twenty years earlier, retailers sold inexpensive furniture by the piece, favoring items of sturdy oak design. During the 1920s, manufacturers expanded their lines of low- and medium-priced furniture, offering wide selections of suites in both

The Hardin-Lavin Company located on Cottage Grove Avenue in Chicago presented this pipeless furnace in the 1920s. The company's Practical Service Department offered to help contractors plan their projects to include the "simplest, most inexpensive, and best method of installation." Bungalows contained modern central heating systems, a marked improvement over wood burning stoves and fireplaces. (American Builder, October 1921.)

period and modern styles. With simple millwork, bungalows accommodated the various new lines of furniture without clashing. Once again, common houses gained complexity by the addition of standard components, in this case, movable objects that varied considerably in style and cost. Home owners could choose furniture that varied in cost and style, arranging and rearranging pieces in a manner they found satisfying.

STANDARDIZATION AND THE UTILITARIAN MARKET: PLUMBING

The manufacturers of millwork created a variety of styles and simple options because homeowners found these choices appealing. During the bungalow boom, the numerous stock patterns of millwork allowed developers of modest neighborhoods to create fashionable environments where interiors and exteriors varied. The evolution of the modern bathroom involved a different process. In the case of plumbing, consumers did not wish to pay a higher price for fashionable fixtures. They preferred less expensive, utilitarian products. Unfortunately, for more than two decades, manufacturers encountered severe problems making modern plumbing fixtures affordable for the masses. In order to do so, they limited options and produced a few standard designs for toilets, sinks, and bathtubs. In 1926, the 70 house designs in the Sears mail order catalog ranged in cost from $4,365 to $986. But the company advertised only two standard bathroom packages. By the 1920s, architects and plumbers claimed that little variation existed in the basic operation of most plumbing fixtures. According to Vandervoort Walsh, all consumers wanted was a toilet with a quick and rapid flush that made its contents disappear before refilling with water.

It took 40 years to develop affordable and reliable modern plumbing. In the United States, the first substantial demand for sanitary ware arose during the 1880s, when new hotels, skyscrapers, and some middle-class households purchased modern systems of plumbing. Contemporaries feared the dangers of connecting residences with the city's sewer system. Consequently, reformers initiated campaigns to make these systems safe and sanitary. They believed that modern plumbing required standardization and simplicity, traits at odds with the practices of many local plumbers who produced complicated and costly installations. Before 1880, the quality of plumbing depended almost exclusively on the judgment, skill, and honesty of tradesmen, whose work demanded an intimate knowledge of metals, since plumbers, at this time, still fashioned their own traps and fittings. A significant breakthrough in plumbing occurred when Caleb Durham developed a system of wrought-iron threaded pipe with recessed fittings that allowed for a smooth continuous surface on the interior of the pipe. The Durham system reduced the cost of labor as well as the time necessary for planning installations. By the twentieth century, major manufacturers of sanitary pipe supplied fittings that became standards in the industry, achieving the goals of reformers by improving safety and reducing the opportunities for fraud by tradesmen who undertook unnecessarily complex installations when simple fittings would suffice.

Despite advances in metal fixtures, the manufacturers of sanitary ware still encountered serious obstacles when they struggled to produce an effective toilet. In 1884, J.L. Mott

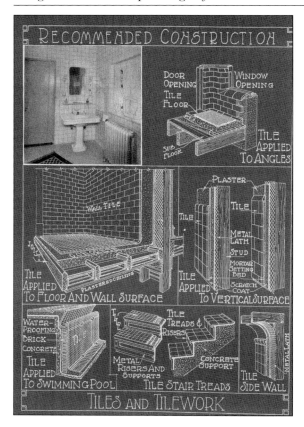

American Builder *magazine provided this plan for tiles and tilework in a modern bathroom. Tiles were seen as an effective way of keeping bathroom areas clean and waterproof.* (American Builder, *December 1921.)*

established a plant in Chicago that provided plumbing fixtures for many of the city's famous buildings, including the Auditorium, the Rookery, the Tacoma, and the Marshall Field Warehouse. The Mott Company began as an iron works. Like its eventual competitors, American Sanitary, Crane, and Kohler, the firm produced a successful line of enameled cast iron bathtubs and sinks. Initially, most of Mott's toilets were mechanical, with arrangements of valves, levers, and plungers, and a combination of ceramic and metal parts. All of the firms that began as iron works relied on outside sources for the pottery used in their fixtures. At first, they imported basins and bowls from England. However, by the 1890s, a handful of small firms in Trenton, New Jersey, became the dominant suppliers of sanitary pottery in the United States.

Regardless of improvements, mechanical toilets encountered problems due to leaks and the lack of a flush adequate to cleanse the bowl and the various mechanical parts. Most schemes to create a workable, modern toilet recognized that a truly sanitary fixture depended upon eliminating metal parts and developing a non-mechanical ceramic water closet that could be cleaned easily and would not absorb urine and waste. During the 1880s, Americans patented various designs for a vitreous toilet with an effective flush that discharged all its contents, cleansed the bowl, and resealed after each flush to retain a water barrier separating the bowl from the discharge pipes that connected the toilet to the sewer system.

The industry achieved a successful design. By 1896, manufacturers generally agreed that a proper modern toilet should be a single piece of vitreous china that employed siphonic action to remove its contents. Unfortunately, they could not produce large numbers of such toilets at an affordable price. The large firms, all former iron works including American Sanitary, Mott, Crane, and Kohler, produced satisfactory cast iron enameled sinks and tubs, but continued to rely on the Trenton potteries for their supplies of non-mechanical ceramic toilets. For more than a decade, the major firms also continued to manufacture and sell an inferior but more affordable line of cast iron enameled toilets.

The manufacture of sanitary ware in Trenton remained a slow, labor-intensive process, controlled by highly skilled, fiercely independent artisans. The most significant workers, the pressers, began with flat sheets of soft clay that they packed, by hand, into plaster of paris moulds. Modern siphon toilets required as many as 16 pieces. After allowing a day for the clay to dry, the presser joined the various pieces, smoothing the joints with a sponge to form a single piece of pottery. A presser learned to make only one or two standard types of toilet. Nevertheless, because of the difficulty of the process, each worker produced only two to five toilets a day.

Once combined, the clay pieces dried for four to six weeks before being prepared for the kiln. The process of firing sanitary ware also required considerable skill, as well as an additional 10 days to complete. The standard beehive kilns were 16 to 18 feet wide and 20 feet high. After individual pieces were encased in a protective clay sagger, the kiln operator stacked each piece carefully in the kiln. Then the kiln was heated slowly to a temperature as high as 2,600 degrees, without the aid of a mechanical gauge. The operator relied on experience to achieve a proper firing. Despite his careful attention to the process, a large portion of the output was unsatisfactory, since toilets had to retain structural integrity on both the interior and exterior of each piece during a prolonged firing of intense heat. If defects escaped the watchful eyes of workmen, the subsequent failures very quickly could ruin the reputation of even the most respected pottery.

After removing the toilets from the kiln, workers finished pieces, correcting defects and filling small cracks. Each toilet then was dipped by hand into a carefully prepared glaze and allowed to dry before being returned to the kilns. A second firing, at equally intense temperatures, fused the glaze and the clay to form the hard, glass-like finish that gave ceramic ware its advantage over more porous materials. Once workers had completed the manufacturing process, skilled packers carefully encased the toilet in wooden crates, cushioning the product with straw to avoid breakage during shipping. Packing often doubled the weight of the product, leading to very high costs for transportation.

Because all ceramic sanitary ware manufacturers depended upon skilled union labor, firms within the industry reached a general agreement in 1895 on prices, wages, and working conditions. The agreement functioned well for more than two decades, preventing ruinous competition among a group of small manufacturers, who did not practice careful methods of cost accounting. Throughout this period, Trenton remained the dominant producer of ceramic toilets. But the financial and technological backwardness of the industry led to a series of challenges. New manufacturing companies developed in the Midwest, many of which did not employ union workers. They also enjoyed lower shipping costs to the nation's most rapidly expanding urban markets. When shipped, a toilet, bathtub, and sink typically weighed more than 1,000 pounds. Not surprisingly, then, a Midwestern firm such as Kohler sold half of its products nearby in Chicago.

In an effort to consolidate the various manufacturing techniques necessary for the production of bathroom fixtures, the larger firms, including Crane and American Standard, developed their own sanitary potteries. These firms recognized that enameled cast iron products could no longer compete with vitreous toilets. When American Sanitary established a substantial pottery in Kokomo, Indiana, the company informed the Trenton firm of Thomas Maddock that it would no longer require a supplier of ceramic sanitary ware. Without a complete line of plumbing products, the independent Trenton manufacturers no longer competed for the large contracts awarded by hotels and office buildings.

The movement toward consolidation changed standard practices in the industry.

This original bungalow bathroom on North Newland exhibits typical white tiles and bathroom fixtures from the 1920s. (Photograph by Mati Maldre.)

Throughout the United States prior to 1910, wholesalers stocked and sold a wide variety of products to plumbers rather than the general public. The complex nature of manufacture and distribution within the industry did not encourage most wholesalers to favor a set of one manufacturer's fixtures over another's. With consolidation, American Sanitary, Mott, Crane, and Kohler concentrated on selling matched sets of toilets, sinks, and bathtubs in various price ranges. In 1914, Mott's catalog offered complete sets that ranged in price from $70 to more than $800. Like millwork manufacturers, Mott aggressively marketed high-end fashionable products, while also selling standard, more utilitarian goods.

Sears, Roebuck challenged the function of wholesalers when the Chicago firm began selling plumbing fixtures directly to consumers. By 1910, the company was selling complete plumbing outfits for as low as $39. Mail order companies were supplied by increasing numbers of new manufacturers, who initiated a more competitive market for fixtures. The most progressive of these firms was Universal Standard Manufacturing of New Castle, Pennsylvania. As early as 1908, Universal Standard experimented with a casting process for pouring liquid clay into dry moulds and with continuous tunnel kilns. Led by C.J. Kirk, Universal Standard attempted to overcome the bottleneck created by unionized pressers and kiln operators in the Trenton shops. Kirk knew that traditional methods of manufacture would not permit a lower selling price, which would increase the market for plumbing fixtures and justify a greater volume of production. Trenton potter Archibald Maddock described Kirk as a genius, who blazed a trail of innovation but "was not a money-making type." In fact, after 15 years of costly experimentation, Kirk's efforts proved most beneficial to larger consolidated firms, such as American Sanitary, Crane, and Kohler. These firms invested in tunnel kilns and casting processes in order to supply the demand for plumbing fixtures during the great bungalow boom of the '20s.

As the boom approached, the more mechanized, non-union shops, such as American Sanitary's Kokomo pottery, had cost advantages of 25 to 33 percent over unionized shops. Nevertheless, Trenton's skilled, union men remained confident that casting and tunnel kilns still possessed serious technical drawbacks. In 1922, after a disastrous strike, the agreements between manufacturers and labor in Trenton ended. The potteries became open shops. Quickly, a few local firms, such as Thomas A. Maddock, switched to casting and installed tunnel kilns. The Maddock pottery's capacity doubled, allowing it to produce 7,000 toilets a week. Despite these improvements, Maddock sold his operation to American Sanitary. As casting and tunnel kilns became the standard methods of production, the gas-fired kilns provided potters with a greater degree of control in producing vitreous bodies, which warped if overheated and cracked if cooled too quickly. The smaller, more traditional firms that had characterized the industry in Trenton could not afford the new methods of production and in rapid succession closed their doors. As a consequence, the number of ceramic sanitary ware manufacturers declined from 35 in 1920 to six in 1940.

Sanitary ware manufacture never automated fully. Instead, the industry simplified its product lines because consumers preferred low-priced, standard, white fixtures. While firms such as Kohler attempted to introduce color and stylishness to the industry, their efforts failed because, as Archibald Maddock maintained, the market for plumbing expanded because of accelerated demand, not the industry's promotional efforts. In nearly

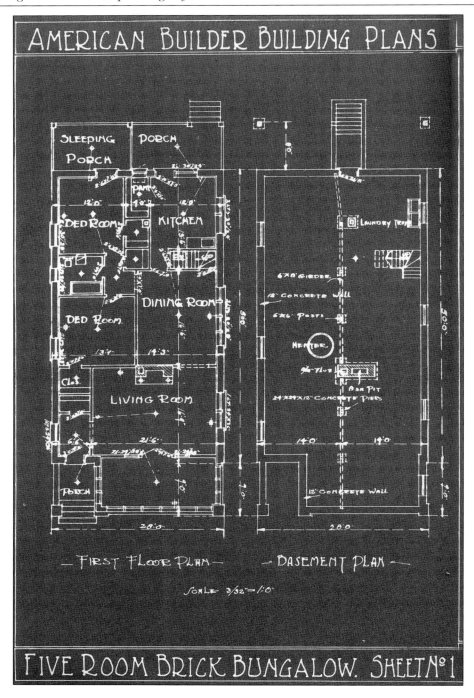

AMERICAN BUILDER BUILDING PLANS

FIVE ROOM BRICK BUNGALOW. SHEET Nº 1

The American Builder *featured these plans for a Chicago-style bungalow as part of its "Street of Beautiful Homes" feature. Notice the simple, open floor plan, the small front porch and the plan for a*

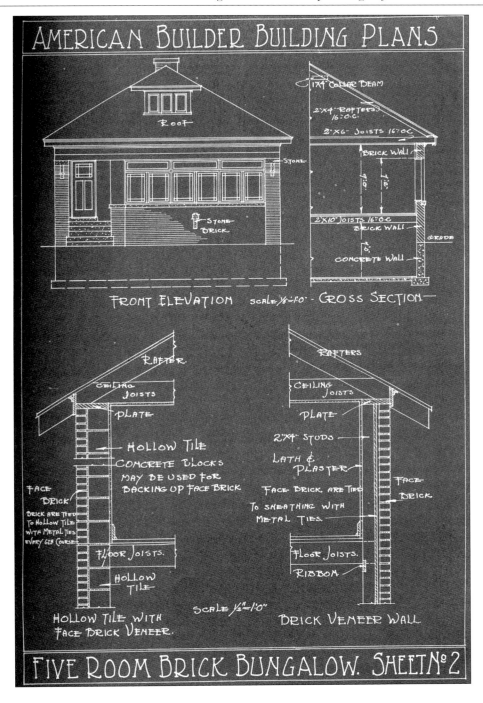

full basement including a laundry area. (American Builder, May 1921.)

all bungalows, bathrooms were small, clean, and utilitarian. At best, bathrooms acquired distinctiveness by variations in tile patterns that offered contrast to the overwhelmingly dominant standard white toilet, sink, and bathtub. Only in a small way did the bathroom add fashion to the common house.

CONCLUSION

During the past decade, historians of American business have shown that during the twentieth century, flexible systems of production allowed smaller manufacturers to respond to consumer desires. No one method of manufacture could possibly supply the elements necessary for even a very modest house. In the case of millwork, local firms expanded rapidly in response to the building boom of the 1880s. The largest of these firms increased their capacity to provide in volume the common products necessary for all houses, while at the same time maintaining the ability to produce items for special orders. Despite such early developments in the industry, no consolidation occurred that would have allowed a few major firms to dominate the production of millwork. Like furniture manufacturers, millwork firms remained modest in size, supplying markets with small batches of standardized but fashionable goods. As a consequence, the industry offered a range of options for even the simplest bungalow.

In contrast, the plumbing industry did not achieve a high level of production until after 1915, when advances in urban water supply and sewer systems led a few major firms to invest in new levels of manufacture that eliminated the bottleneck caused by a dependence on highly skilled workers. During the great bungalow boom of the '20s, these manufacturers consolidated and standardized rapidly. In larger, more mechanized factories, they produced a narrow range of high-volume, affordable products whose styles and operation differed in only minor ways. Cleanliness became fashionable. Variations in bathroom fixtures did not.

The bungalow, then, derived from complex origins. In most cases, the basic floor plan evolved from nineteenth century Chicago working-class houses that had improved over 40 years of residential development. Slowly, new methods of manufacture had allowed for greater elaboration, both inside and outside the traditional structure. In addition, as immigrant communities Americanized and as the middle ranks of society increased their income, they exercised their tastes more liberally. National advertisers who wished to create demand and encourage spending influenced their choices. Certainly, the furniture industry supplied and aggressively marketed an increasing variety of stylish goods, affordable especially with credit. However, in plumbing, heating, and electrical supply, manufacturers limited variety to make products affordable. The bungalow became the ubiquitous house in Chicago's first market for modern housing, the basic building block in a city of neighborhoods. By combining affordable artistry and affordable comfort so successfully, it also proved to be one of the city's most significant contributions to twentieth-century architecture.

three

BUILDING AND SELLING CHICAGO'S BUNGALOW BELT

by Charles Shanabruch

Developers created whole communities at one time on the vacant land at Chicago's edge forming a continuous belt of bungalows. These bungalows along Marquette Road across from Marquette Park are part of the Chicago Bungalow Belt. (Photograph by Mati Maldre.)

etween 1910 and 1930, the rate of growth in the City of Chicago was unexcelled by any other major American city. Chicagoans built nearly 80,000 bungalows and more than twice as many apartment units to house its ever-growing population. While the population grew from 2.4 million to 3.4 million, the number of housing units built was even more impressive as people sought to have their own space in the city. This dramatic growth in single-family houses resulted from families seeking to flee congested neighborhoods and own their own homes and from the success of a sales force with the proper tools to make the dream a reality. Developers who subdivided land, builders and their contractors who constructed the houses, and financial institutions that lent the money all contributed essential elements. The pattern of the residential development process does not appear to have been uniform, but there was a clear evolution in patterns of subdivision, construction, sales, and financing of Chicago's housing in the two decades of greatest growth.

LAND DEVELOPMENT

From the beginning, Chicagoans speculated in land. In the hope of making a substantial profit, land speculators purchased land and then resold it to others who would develop and build the city. The close relationship between speculation and the development of the city emerged when Chicago was just an outpost. Chicago area land was auctioned off in New York in anticipation of the Illinois and Michigan Canal replacing the Chicago River portage and fueled Chicago's first land boom between 1830 and 1842. Land increased in value almost daily as speculators seized the opportunity to make a profit by buying and reselling the promise of Chicago's ascent from the mud flats along the Chicago River. Railroad development in the late 1840s through the 1850s fueled subsequent booms. The city's development as the depot for the nation's breadbasket increased the economic vitality and swelled the city's population after the Civil War through the cataclysmic fire in 1871. The prosperous times in the nation at large and Chicago in particular produced a land boom between 1878 and 1898. In anticipation of the continued growth, speculators purchased land at the city's edge and began to subdivide it.

By 1890, more than a million people called Chicago home. The belief that the Columbian Exposition would be held in Chicago further ignited land speculation, drove up prices, and produced a new wave of subdivision activity. Chicago's population increased rapidly as immigrants from Europe filled the factories and heightened demand for apartments, tenements, and single-family housing. Residential districts continued to expand outward as did the city boundaries. The boom of the 1890s, however, ended abruptly, and subdivided land sat vacant waiting for the next wave of optimism and surge in population.

While the speculative mania waned in the 20-year period after the great fair, the city continued to grow, using up land that had had been subdivided in some of the outlying districts. New manufacturing districts pushed the residential areas further and further from the core, and the use of streetcars and the completion of the elevated system caused the city's population and housing stock to spread out. Home ownership, while the dream of many, was the lot of few, especially the immigrants who crowded together in the substandard housing in the industrial area. While residential housing development began to take place in a systematic way to house industrial workers, most remained in tenements near the factories where they labored.

A review of City of Chicago Building Department permits issued in the spring of 1915 indicates a preponderance of apartment buildings being constructed. Two to six flats were the dominant product being permitted. Nonetheless, permits were issued for individuals who were building single homes or more. For example, that April *The Economist* recorded that architect Jesse E. Schiller had designed a two-story stucco house to cost $5,000 and four one-story "bungalows" to be erected by E.L. Sommers in Dauphine Park that would cost $3,000 each.

In the 1915 edition that was devoted to the previous year's highlights and forecasts for the new one, *The Economist* reported on land acquisitions and noted "operators are buying outlying acres with a view to meeting a normal demand for houses and lots." It believed people who operated in vacant lands were "among the shrewdest class in the market and have the growth of the city in population and the demand figured out to a nicety and know what they can do with a piece of property before they buy it." Indeed, the City of Chicago Building Department showed an "active" market in the recent past. The same pattern existed in the adjoining municipalities as well.

At Oak Park and Austin Avenues, Burt P. Biggs, a real estate broker and developer, purchased 45 acres from Henry W. Austin, President of Oak Park Trust and Savings Bank, for $100,000 with the intention of subdividing it into 300 lots with 30- to 50-feet frontages. Biggs planned to call his development Oaks Terrace, spend $10,000 in landscaping, and require 25-foot setbacks. On the Southwest Side, John M. Clark, former president of the Chicago Telephone Company, bought 40 acres near Archer and 51st Street for immediate subdivision.

Owners who had speculated in land and saw values plummet in the last building cycle now put it back on the market, making it available to developers. The bust cycle that had began in 1894 finally ended in 1914, when demand for new lots began the cycle of subdividing once again. For example, in spring of 1915, T*he Economist* carried an advertisement for 80 acres "ripe for subdivision," at North Avenue and Harlem. The owner who resided in California sought $1,250 an acre.

Land values in 20 districts that would become the Bungalow Belt remained relatively cheap compared to the areas recently developed nearer to the city's core. In this crescent from the South Shore to Norwood Park, land was mostly vacant and sold for $1,000 to $1,500 an acre if not subdivided or $5–15 a front foot for lots that were approximately 30 by 125 feet, or $150 to $450.

After World War I, when the need for housing became ever more obvious; the time was truly ripe for development. The Chicago newspapers devoted considerable attention to the housing shortage. Noting that the war had stopped residential construction, *The Economist* estimated a shortage of one million houses nationally. Nearly 1.1 million young men reached the age of 21 and one million reached the age of 25, and these young men married and needed homes. The resumption of immigration in 1919 added even more pressure. "The laboring classes of the United States are entitled to decent housing facilities," the editor argued.

"Own-Your Home" Movement

Housing America's families was a matter of grave national concern, but real estate developers viewed it as an opportunity. The situation grew to near crisis proportions immediately after the war in Europe. Workers flocked to urban areas and the return of tens of thousands of soldiers who began to have families created a crisis that gave birth to the "Own Your Home" movement. On April 6, 1919, *The Chicago Tribune* noted that the steep advance in rents resulted in considerable hardship for persons of moderate means. In fact, in the face of spiraling rents, young families returned home to live with their parents. In Springfield, the legislature even pondered imposing rent controls to prevent gouging. The cost of renting a flat in Chicago nearly doubled between 1919 and 1924. The increased rents made owning a home an attractive option both as a release from high rents and the discomforts of flat life. "This in itself," *The Chicago Tribune* noted, "is a most wholesome sign, as it long has been recognized that flat life does not make for the best class of citizenship, besides the unfavorable conditions created for the proper rearing of children."

The National Association of Real Estate Boards, working with their membership, promoted expositions to support and encourage the idea of home ownership as well as to provide local builders and building suppliers an opportunity to demonstrate new ideas in construction. In spring 1920, the Chicago Board of Realtor's Own Your Home Committee, led by William Britigan, a successful real estate developer and builder, sponsored its first exposition at the Chicago Coliseum. As the movement grew so did its promotional agenda. By 1922, the committee grew to include city and suburban builders as well as architects, landscape architects, vendors, and representatives of the public utilities. By 1923, another prominent developer and builder, William Zelosky, chaired the program, which had 22 active committees and 10 specialized sub-committees such as brick, wallpaper and coverings, metal lath, paint, and varnish and other building products.

For the Third Annual Exposition, the Board of Realtors planned to build within the Coliseum a full-sized bungalow completely furnished so that all could see the latest ideas in construction, furnishings, and design. The bungalow was the work of R.C. Spencer, Chairman of the Architectural Committee, and represented the "best small home planning ideas" of the participating architects. There were five primary rooms on the first floor and the potential to build out two more on the second floor. Owing to the difficulty of handling the expected crowds, only the first floor of the Chicago Coliseum structure was furnished. Interesting features included a refrigerator placed in an entryway just off the rear porch with doors to permit both inside and outside icing. The bungalow was designed so that rear porch could be enlarged for dining, and a bay window with window seats and a fireplace made the living room attractive and warm. Chicago's leading interior decorators and a large furniture merchandiser combined forces to create an attractive living space. The bungalow's exterior was white ivory stucco with gray-green trim around the widows.

Because the setting of the bungalow was so important, the landscape and garden committee made plans to reproduce this bungalow in miniature to scale in the midst of a lawn and garden to give it the "perfect setting." Thus, the committee hoped that the

*The "Own Your Own Home" Movement was both a social and economic crusade. Real estate interests joined with social and civic groups to promote home ownership, especially for families. (*American Builder, *December 1919.)*

visitors would be able to see the completely furnished full-size home as well as "to visualize the complete house—house, lawn and garden." Ralph R. Root of Root & Hollister landscape architects cooperated with the nurserymen subcommittee and the Allied Florists Association and the Woman's Farm and Garden Association.

The Exposition included three large exhibits. The City of Chicago Zoning Commission, which sought the opportunity to explain its proposed legislation for residential districts to prospective home buyers, presented the first one. Additionally, exhibits of home plans and sketches and landscape gardening were displayed to help people with ideas for their own homes. The committee offered individual vendors and builders exposition space but tightly control who would exhibit in order to eliminate "irresponsible and unreliable firms." Nearly 150,000 people attended the exposition to view recent advances in building amenities and to learn about home sites offered by exhibitors.

Promotion of home ownership became a national mission. The Better Homes in America movement, initiated in 1922, with President Calvin Coolidge as honorary chairman and Secretary of Commerce Herbert Hoover as chairman, drew upon civic groups and government agencies such as the United States Children's Bureau to lend support. On Chicago's Southwest Side, the Clearing Welfare Club and the Clearing Women's Club heeded the call and built a model bungalow at 5501 West 64th Street that "would be an inspiration and education to those who already own their homes and to those who should some day achieve this forward character making ambition." On June 20, 1925, the two organizations laid the cornerstone of an attractive bungalow and in the dedication brochure stated: "We realize with the National Government that the home is the foundation of our nation, and it is our desire to promote better home building and home life in this section making it a better community to live in and in which to raise our children."

Charles Ringer—South Shore

The development of the Bungalow Belt was contingent on the work of entrepreneurs who committed their time and funds in getting to know an area well and using all of their powers of persuasion to secure a return on that investment. A new breed of subdividers emerged and helped to create the Bungalow Belt. One of these was Charles Ringer, who developed land and sold real estate in South Shore.

In 1900, at a time of depressed land values, Ringer established his real estate office. The Columbian Exposition had led to a boom on the South Side, but when the dreams of speculators and investors did not materialize, land values collapsed. At the time Ringer started his business, real estate dealers were considered to be unfortunates who could not find other means of employment. Not dissuaded by the negative climate, the young Ringer opened his office at 79th Street and Exchange near the Illinois Central Railroad station. He put up a large sign that proclaimed his name and his business in real estate, mortgages, and fire insurance and his specialization in "South Shore, Windsor Park And Cheltenham Property."

Ringer viewed the real estate business as more than simply executing transactions.

This view of 77th and Jeffrey looking south in 1915 shows Jeffrey Boulevard as a dirt road and portrays a country scene. Much of the land in Chicago lay undeveloped before the 1920s. (Courtesy of Special Collections and Preservation Division, Chicago Public Library.)

This photograph, looking south from 77th and Jeffrey taken in 1934, shows the results of the housing expansion of the 1920s. Instead of a dirt road lined with trees, Jeffrey is a city street lined with bungalows and apartment buildings. Our Lady of Peace Catholic Church stands in the background. (Courtesy of Special Collections and Preservation Division, Chicago Public Library.)

Rather, he engaged in community development and became a civic booster, fighting for the laying of sewers and sidewalks along 79th Street, the building of new schools and feeder bus lines. He grew his business and, when the opportunity to purchase the Windsor Park Golf Course, an 80-acre piece of land bounded by 75th and 79th Streets and Yates and Colfax, presented itself, he purchased and prepared to subdivide the land. Ringer promoted the location as only 25 minutes from downtown by the Illinois Central Railroad with surface lines on both 75th and 79th Streets, access to South Shore Drive, and within walking distance to the Lake Michigan Beach, South Shore Country Club, and Jackson Park. More importantly, he promoted the development as home to "the best class of people. . . such as officials of Steel Companies, Banks and Railroads." His brochure touted the excellent schools and the variety of churches, including: Methodist, Baptist, Presbyterian, Episcopal, Congregational, Catholic, English and German-speaking Lutheran, and Swedish Lutheran and Methodist.

Ringer did not market his subdivision to the end user but the investor who would buy the land and hold it for appreciation and resale and for the builder who had a buyer or built in hopes of finding a buyer. It was this latter group that Ringer sought most particularly. He called their attention to investment value: "We are selling lots on a basis that *must* (emphasis added) yield a profit to the buyers." To facilitate the sale of land Ringer required only 25 percent down at the time of signing.

To ensure that his users would have the certainty they needed in building and investing, he placed restrictions on all land sold. Land along 75th and 79th Streets would be for commercial use. Ringer reserved a portion of the subdivision for apartments, "modern in every respect, but altogether in their own district." Most importantly, a section devoted exclusively to residences would have generous 40-foot-wide lots with a guarantee that there would be no shops, businesses, or apartments. Emphasizing that the buyer could count on no changes in use "as restrictions on these buildings prohibit the possibility of a shack being placed along side a home. The restrictions protect the rights of all classes of investors and sacrifice no class at the expense of the other." Also reassuring was the requirement that all residences might not be erected for less than $5,000.

Charles Ringer promised the project was to be "the last word in perfect subdivisions," with the best improvements possible. He offered his land for sale at prices beginning at $60 a front foot in August 1919, with improvements to be installed so construction could begin in January 1920. The residential lots sold out in only three-and-a-half days! Ringer bought "another tract" of 20 acres further south at 81st and Colfax for $435,000, to be improved for "160 bungalows to retail at moderate prices," but soon sold it to J. Ogden Armour who planned to move the Armour Institute (Illinois Institute of Technology) to South Shore.

Charles Ringer did not work alone in the South Shore community. Twelve other real estate offices of varying sizes and expertise joined in the sale of South Shore properties. Among them were Woodrich Brothers, Peter Foote Company, James A. Malooly, James G. Barsaaux, Inc., Carroll Schendorf & Boenickke, McKey & Pogue Inc., John E. Nelson, Ed. G. Laughlin, Glatt & Price, Hamilton Brothers, Swanson and House, and Wagner Brothers. However, the most successful appeared to be the South Shore Investment Company with offices on 75th Street. Established in 1923 by John A Carroll, the owner of banks in Hyde Park, South Shore, and South Chicago, along with a New York partner, the company paid $1,000,000 for the land that J. Ogden Armour had purchased from Charles Ringer months earlier. Through aggressive promotion, the South Shore Investment Company sold all of the parcels at a total price of $2,750,000 within three months. The company put in and paid for all improvements, including street, sewer, water, sidewalks, gas, and electricity with the lots.

BRITIGAN—SOUTH AND SOUTHWEST SIDES

While Ringer developed South Shore, William H. Britigan made a mark both further west and further south. In 1917, Britigan sold more than 2,500 lots with a vale in excess of $4 million. After the war he continued his development efforts, and in April 1919, The William Britigan Organization announced the sale of its lots in Marquette Manor. With three subdivision offices located at 63rd and Western, 63rd and California, and 59th and Kedzie, Britigan offered the whole subdivision for sale on Sunday and Monday April 4th and 5th. An advertisement in *The Chicago Tribune* blared: "GREAT CLOSING SALE," and noted that the price for all remaining lots would be raised "substantially" on Tuesday. "In

William Britigan developed property in all sections of the city. Notice how his logo played on the patriotic impulses and civic spirit of the "Own Your Own Home Movement." (Olcott's Land Values, 1923.)

the history of Chicago there has never been offered to the people a more valuable opportunity than in MARQUETTE MANOR. What was a few years ago farm land today has been developed into a high class residential subdivision, and no money was spared to accomplish the purpose and to make this property the finest home spot on the great Southwest Side." The copy ended with the advice "DON"T WAIT!"

In June 1919, Britigan purchased 60 acres of land between 67th and 71st Streets between Western and Rockwell for $250,000, and sold them out in lots by the end of the year. Within months, he purchased 100 acres between 95th and 99th Streets and Michigan Avenue and South Park Boulevard and subdivided it to meet the "urgent" demand for homes in that section. He named the subdivision Bermont Manor to give it a suburban feel and "restricted" it to residential usage requiring a 20-foot setback and required a minimum cost of $4,000 per unit. Britigan's strategy emphasized the ease of accessibility from all of the important South Side factory districts served by cross town and downtown surface lines and its nearness to the Illinois Central Burnside Station.

Zelosky—North and Northwest Sides

The success of Ringer's organization in South Shore was exceeded by William Zelosky on the city's Northwest Side. His newspaper advertisements heralded "A Home of Your Own," with a picture of a bungalow and the promise of 30 years experience in the real estate business. William Zelosky came to the United States as an immigrant from Poland in 1893, and a year later opened his own real estate business. His hard work and vision paid off despite the collapse in real estate prices. Within 30 years, Zelosky's company had lots, two-flats, and homes for sale and under development in the City of Chicago and Oak Park, as he chaired the Chicago Real Estate Board's "Own Your Home" committee. Among his developments were the Addison Addition (Addison near the Ravenswood elevated); North Kenilworth Boulevard Addition in Oak Park; Colonial Gardens (Lawrence and Central) and Park View Crest (Devon and Austin). While Zelosky maintained his central office in the heart of downtown, he served his clients from 10 branch offices in the neighborhoods. Eight offices were on the Northwest Side, including four offices along Milwaukee Avenue, and additional offices were located at 3806 West 63rd Street in a fast developing section of the Southwest Side and in the Village of Oak Park. In 30 years, he built his one-person office to an organization of 400 sales and office personnel.

Zelosky targeted each subdivision to different markets. The Addison Addition was near the Lincoln and Irving streetcars as well as the Ravenswood line. It featured "two-apartment" brick homes. The addition had room for 500 units and targeted people leaving the density and blight of older neighborhoods with frame buildings. A promotional piece stressed that his homes were brick and did not need the maintenance of wood buildings, "In our opinion the best external material for buildings in the Chicago region is brick." Likewise, Zelosky touted the quality of the investment, noting that lots that had sold for $7–800 when the subdivision opened now sold for 3–500 percent more. He believed that the reason for the enduring and increasing value was the guarantee of a stable

Courtesy Cleveland Plan Commission.

Most Cities Look Like This Conglomerate Group in a Public Street Car. No Similarity—Nothing but Jarring Association.

*This cartoon calls attention to the problems common to all cities where absence of restrictions on land use created uncomfortable situations for homeowners. Chicago introduced zoning laws, mandatory restrictions, in 1923 so that this would not occur again. (*American Builder, *October 1921.)*

environment created by the restrictions that required residential uses.

Zelosky based all of his projects upon the evolving wisdom regarding land use restrictions. As early as 1909, a speaker to the American Civic Association, in a speech entitled "The Beautifying of Cities," noted that subdivision restrictions were no longer to be considered a matter for "high-class sections, where only the man of means was able to select a home site and because of his means was able to protect himself against the future." The speaker explained that the time had come to create subdivisions for the "modest workman" that would provide "restrictions as to the nature of construction that will be permitted in that section, and restrictions that will preserve that district along the lines of homelike beauty." Zelosky promised that his subdivisions would not become unsightly and ugly causing values to depreciate. Rather, when he subdivided the land he made covenants regarding restrictions a part of the deed of conveyance.

The Oak Park subdivision was not for modest workingmen, but for the more affluent buyer seeking suburban conveniences. Prior to putting the project on the market, Zelosky spent $150,000 in improvements for trellis and gates with architectural monuments at the boulevard entrance. Asphalt streets, cement curbs and sidewalks, sewers, water mains, and gas mains were constructed through out the property. Yet while older sections of Oak Park commanded $150 per front foot, Zelosky's prices began at $40.

Zelosky made a major commitment in the area served by the new Ravenswood transit line when he purchased the Hopkin and Garden farms in 1916. Bounded by Lawrence and Foster and Austin and Central Avenues, he subdivided it into over 1,200 home sites. This was his first effort to zone land for three uses: residence, apartments, and business. His literature proclaimed; "Colonial Gardens has no bungalow sandwiched in between an apartment building or an apartment building between bungalows." He allocated 80 acres to residences, 70 acres to apartments, and the remainder to streets and businesses. This project had a very slow start; by 1922, it had only 100 residences.

Further north and west, he purchased a 60-acre tract at Devon that ran southeasterly along the Forest Preserve to Austin. He named this subdivision of nearly 500 lots "Park View Crest." "Picture in your mind," his brochure said, " a crest of land laying 40 feet above and overlooking a several hundred acre plateau well-wooded with all species of wild trees in this region and every kind of wild fruit tree, and in season wild birds and flowers in abundance, the most ideal place for a home where your children have the benefit to grow up among the trees, birds, and flowers and enjoy pure air and sunshine. All this natural beauty will be preserved by the State Forest Commission." If the promise of nature were not enough, Zelosky appealed to avarice saying that the buyer "may never again have so good an opportunity" for such a land value increase.

BUNGALOWS

on lots 40x172 feet

IN THIS DISTRICT

Small Cash Payment - Easy Monthly Payments

Have You Customers ?

If so phone me and earn a commission

J. E. WHITE

SUBDIVIDER AND BUILDER

139 N. Clark Street, Phone Central 3295
Suites 1505-8

Developers and subdividers such as J.E. White used a variety of methods to reach clients to purchase his 20-acre subdivision at 83rd and Cottage Grove. This ad appeared in Olcott's Land Values Blue Book *in order to attract real estate agents and builders who relied on this publication for tracking land values on each block in the city annually. (Olcott's Land Values, 1923.)*

ARCHITECTS AND BUILDERS

Most bungalow builders were not part of a large organization, rather they were independent contractors who purchased land from sub-dividers, hired an architect, and contracted for the services that they needed. The range of designs and the styles and detailing in the bungalows are a reflection of the unique process that was used in the building of the Bungalow Belt.

A tour of the bungalow neighborhoods gives the impression that many of the bungalows came from stock plans published by blueprint houses; however, many architects did design for specific builders and end users. Builders seemed to have had architects stamp stock plans in many instances and then added their own distinguishing details in the brickwork and windows. *The Economist* listed the building permits issued weekly and identified architects and costs. Some examples follow. J.E. Scheller designed a one-story bungalow, 26.8 by 83.2 feet of pressed brick and stone with hot water heat and a garage 19.6 by 20.9 feet for about $9,000. Earnest N. Braucher of 6 North Clark drew plans for R.A. Cepek real estate at 5 North LaSalle for "two more brick bungalows, 23 by 40 and 24 by 41 with furnace heat," to be constructed on East 85th Street near Stony Island for a combined total of $13,000. Braucher also signed plans for three brick bungalows, "each 24 by 52.6 with hot water heat to be built in Norwood Park at a total cost of $19,500." Dewey and Pavloick, architects at 4804 North Kedzie, took commissions for more elaborate bungalows. They drew plans up for B. Zeches for two six-room bungalows, 28 by 75 feet with two-car garages in Evanston, to be constructed at a cost of $16,000 each and a larger bungalow at an undisclosed location that was to be 28 by 91 feet with a tile roof and at a cost of $22,000.

Individuals could buy their own lots, select stock plans, and find a builder. Often the prospective bungalow owner would go to the lumberyard to buy plans and materials and hire a general contractor to manage the carpenters, plumbers, and masons. Newspapers carried large display advertisements by companies such as Bosley Brothers Lumber, which offered materials and plans for bungalows. In a company advertisement announcing a "May Sale," there were sketches of two bungalows: the "Bentley" and the "Shelley." Plans and materials for the five-room Bentley were $1,495, and the six-room Shelly were $1,620. Brick and labor were additional. Bosley's advertisement noted that it had "hundreds of plans for 4, 5, 6, and 7-room homes, bungalows, and cottages" to be built of brick, frame, or stucco.

Other notices did not identify the architect but noted the builders. For example, Claude E. Anderson, a real estate dealer at 75th and Halsted who had built a number of South Side bungalows, received permits to build several more in the vicinity of Fairfield and West 58th Street at a price of $3,700 each. The notice of the permit identified the subcontractors or noted the opportunity to bid on the work.

The Chicago foreign language newspapers also carried notices of permits. In the *Dziennik Zwiazkowy*, announcements of building permits noted that members of the Polish National Alliance were the masons and carpenters on the construction projects of Polish builders. In South Shore, five dwellings were being erected at 84th and Colfax, with the masonry contract awarded to Z.F. Jakubowski and the carpentry contract to T. Kosculski.

The rewards to land developers and builders were greatest as the demand for housing increased; however, there were also risks that concerned the business community. One analyst in 1922 expressed concern about the climate for building. While noting the demand for housing was intense, he cautioned a boom could not be sustained if the "insurgent building trades unions" were not checked. He warned that capital would not risk large sums of money if it knew that prices for buildings were inflated. "And you can't expect the owner of vacant land to plan improvements when he knows that in a few years an economic law will sweep away artificial restrictions they [unions] seek to impose, reduce costs, and leave him with a building which on an actual basis is worth much less than he built it for." Chicago's Chamber of Commerce worked to outlaw closed shops and set wage scales. As the building season began, builders and businesses joined forces to break strikes by importing workers from outside the metropolitan area. In once instance, builders with the support of the Chamber imported 1,400 journeymen plumbers to break the local union and send a message to the other trades unions.

The post-war prices for construction reached a new level. In 1923, the Chicago *Realtor* printed an article entitled, "Why Houses Cost More," which explained that increases in labor as well as materials, especially lumber, created a new permanent level of pricing for housing. The *Realtor* advised anyone who thought of postponing construction until prices were down to the 1913 level to "incorporate the specifications in his will because they will probably not be carried out in his lifetime."

SALES

The outlook for real estate men was excellent after World War I. In 1921, *The Economist* remarked that real estate men never had better prospects. The opportunities were available for all members of the industry from land subdivider, contractor, broker, and agent as well as mortgage salesmen.

The selling of both subdivision lots and individual homes took on a carnival atmosphere. However, the underlying forces were the desires of people to move out of the city's cramped quarters and overcrowded apartment flats to spaces with more light and space. The opportunity to build housing for this pent up demand was great, and it attracted both the honorable and the not so honorable builder. A developer with a 640-acre subdivision to sell on Belmont Avenue advertised: "Wanted –Subdivision men. . . . A cleanup for hustlers." A developer with four Beverly Hills subdivisions promised, "A big cleanup for live wires." Clearly, these ads in issues of *The Chicago Tribune* in 1924 do not emphasize professional qualifications. In fact, the lack of professionalism was a matter of concern for some who formed real estate boards to monitor and improve the image of the people in the field. For example, in the South Shore district, the bull market between 1922 and 1926 produced an era of prosperity for everyone associated with the trade. However, according to Morgan L Fitch, a realtor for Charles Ringer and President of the South Shore Chamber of Commerce, noted that riding the wave of prosperity were "scores of

Charles Ringer, pictured here in 1926, had his sales staff use the auto as a tool for selling real estate. Often the agents met prospects at the elevated line and drove them to the subdivision. (Courtesy of Special Collections and Preservation Division, Chicago Public Library.)

untutored and self-style real estate experts." The most successful realtors joined together to form the South Shore Real Estate Board and elected James A. Malooly, a broker with offices on Stony Island Avenue, its president with the charge to professionalize the business.

The selling of subdivisions became a science. Eugene Brown told the readers of *Chicago Realtor* some of the tricks of the trade he had developed as well as some pitfalls to avoid. Planning should be done in the fall so that selling could begin at the first of the year, when people tried to keep their resolutions and when they got raises or some account is paid off. Brown advised, "The blood is young in January and people are looking forward to doing big things. They will make decisions then." Picking the "right" subdivision name was essential as well. He noted that an uninteresting name was a handicap and counseled that it was worth the time and expense of replatting the property under a new name. While there were plenty of names, only one was the best and the developer should find it and use it. "As long as a name sounds bad to me, I don't use it. I get one which sounds good the more I say it."

Developers needed to create interest and excitement when announcing their projects. Brown advised his audience that articles should be placed in local papers and should be "devoid of all earmarks of paid advertisement, if possible." He suggested that every occasion that could be incorporated into an announcement, such as street extensions and paving, lighting installations, or property changing hands be used to good effect. Letters and small classified ads that prompted replies from persons interested in buying followed the announcements. Brown explained that good letters and ads emphasized that the "opening" was the best time to buy. He recommended sustaining the barrage of letters and small ads until three days before the sale to get a good list of prospects and to secure some advance sales ready for opening day.

As the sales campaign began, the ads must give more and more information with pictures of homes and then maps of the section of the city near the subdivision. As the sales day approached, he recommended that handbills with details showing lot sizes, prices, and terms be distributed to every house within a 2-mile radius of the subdivision. Each lot was to be marked clearly with details including price and terms, owner, office, and address. In order to "pep up" the site, he recommended gay color pennants 6 feet long on 8-foot-high poles spaced 40 feet apart along the street, but he warned against too much reliance on the stars and stripes.

Closing was the all-important part of the transaction. Here Brown stressed simplicity. If the property were good and the advertisements effective, the salesperson did not have much to do but to show the property. He suggested that salesmen be uniformed with white hats and white suits or wear prominent colored ribbons and be equipped with order forms. Salesmen completed the order forms on the spot and sought the prospect signature. This "promise to pay" made the offer a serious matter but gave the owner the freedom to accept or reject it. In order to hurry up sales, the following rules were used: "First on the lot has first right to purchase," and "No lots held without a deposit." When sales were done from the office, the rule changed to be the "first person to the plat with the required down payment gets the preference." "Official Plat" maps hung in the office to manage the information and to create a sense of competition for the lots. In order to promote quick sales, unsightly lots were to be held back for a later sale.

The sale of real estate was a high-pressure business. Developers put together sophisticated advertising schemes that played on the imagination of persons seeking to leave the congestion of the city and improve their standing among their friends and families. Simultaneously, the message conveyed was that investment in a house in a particular neighborhood was not a matter of speculation but of wise use of resources.

The advertisement that William Britigan placed in *The Chicago Tribune* on Sunday, April 4, 1919, contained all of the elements of the new sales program. Photos of the land and examples of houses to be built were on all four corners of the quarter-page advertisement with the urgent message that the purchase be completed "today or tomorrow," before the buyer faced increased prices. His corporate logo, an eagle with spread wings perched atop the corporate name, tied patriotism and the organization together. Accessibility to employment was touted: "Great Industries Surround Marquette Manor for Miles."

The security of the investment was essential, and the ads promised: "A Lot Is an Investment—Not a Speculation." The fine print noted, "Chicago real estate has already made a thousand fortunes for its owners. . . and will continue this process as long as this city continues to be the metropolis of the great Central West." Britigan asked the prospective buyer to look at the purchase as an investment in Chicago itself, where each decade hundreds of thousands of new people would sustain demand and increase real estate values.

Britigan assured the buyers that their purchase was part of more than a subdivsion development. The stories of people buying lots in distant prairies caused some to hesitate. The explanation captioned "Marquette Manor Not Vacant Prairie," emphasized that the subdivision lay "miles within the city limits," and not in an undeveloped district. "Scores of bungalows and flats have been erected here" giving Marquette Manor a substantial population today, the ad noted.

Equally as important as the quality of the investment and its location was the pricing. Here too, the developer did not fail to address the concerns of the buyer. With hyperbole, the advertisement read:

You Buy a Lot Today Under Market

Come out today and you will be convinced that you can make money by purchasing now at our extremely low prices. When you see MARQUETTE MANOR, you will know how valuable it is. You will appreciate that the millions of dollars which have been spent on this property has made every lot an honest investment, and that our prices are under the real worth of the property.

Finally, the advertisement issued a call to action: "COME OUT TODAY OR TOMORROW." The new element of the sales pitch was the help offered. "WE WILL CALL for YOU with OUR AUTOMOBILE." Britigan told buyers that they could call one of the three offices at the site, and the company would dispatch an automobile to make the trip to Marquette Manor comfortable. He also included detailed instructions for those using surface lines.

The Marquette Manor sales strategy continued Britigan's practice of using the latest in technology and psychology. In 1917, when he sold 2,629 lots he used the services of 53 employees who made 169,000 telephone calls, 1,399,835 pieces of advertising, and 5,000 automobile trips. According to Homer Hoyt, who tracked the value of land in Chicago, sophisticated sales organizations trained their staffs to use the automobile, the telephone, and widespread advertising and promotional gimmicks such as free train rides and free lunches.

Charles Ringer's well-appointed office in 1927 had the real estate agents' newest prospecting tool, the telephone. (Courtesy of Special Collections and Preservation Division, Chicago Public Library.)

FINANCING THE BUNGALOW

The new methods of selling real estate relied upon access to new financing tools to ensure that the persons of moderate means would be able to leave the flats and tenements. Access to capital with manageable terms was essential to support the "Own Your Home" campaign. In order to help the renters, builders and developers had to create the financing mechanisms that would enable a person to buy a home for the cost of renting. Builders met the challenge. In the first building season after World War I, an advertisement in the real estate section of *The Chicago Tribune* offered home seekers a brick bungalow, valued at $4,600 and located at 5649 South Artesian, for only $100 down and with a monthly payment of $25 plus interest.

Developers and builders helped their prospects to secure first mortgages of up to 50 percent of the value of the house, the limit of banks on residential lending. They then worked with the buyer to secure a second mortgage through mortgage brokers, or they provided the second mortgage themselves to ensure the sale of the property. As the building boom grew nationally, insurance companies and others began to underwrite bonds that would be used to support the demand for credit that could not be provided by the restrictive banking industry. Additionally, immigrants and their children developed building and loan associations as a tool to help their members to leave the ports of entry and purchase real estate. These associations were not as highly regulated as banks and made loans to their members for 60 or 70 percent of the purchase price of a home. Finally, new banks were created in the sections of the city where the greatest construction was in progress. Realtors seeking to tap funds for their ventures and their prospective home buyers often became the most active bank investors.

Where credit was difficult to obtain, builders and developers created their own solutions to meet the need for credit. In South Shore, for example, there were few satisfactory agencies for second mortgage financing. Brokers found that Loop brokers charged excessively high rates and provided "impersonal" and "disinterested" service from inconvenient offices. Accordingly, a group of real estate brokers, developers, and investors formed the South Shore Securities Company in 1925, with the express purpose to make second mortgages in South Shore. Among the founding members of the South Shore Securities Company were members of the real estate industry, including Charles Ringer and Peter Foote. Capitalized with $50,000, the company grew rapidly and four years later had $150,000 in common stock and $100,000 in preferred stock four years later. Morgan L Fitch, a Ringer associate, served as president and expanded operations from a small second-floor office to prosperous quarters on East 75th Street.

The company's 1929 annual report stated that as soon as it opened its doors, local contractors and real estate men "swamped" the office. The businessmen proved "eager to do business with a mortgage organization who understood the community and who were pioneering the idea that dealings in junior mortgages were a matter of good business." In its first quarter, South Shore Securities Company issued $70,000 in second mortgages. By the last quarter of 1928, it had invested nearly $500,000 in second mortgages and planned to issue an additional $100,000 in stock to accommodate "moderate expansion" in the demand for housing.

The use of first and second mortgages worked at the outset of the land development but had severe limitations. The first mortgages were offered at rates of four percent to six percent on up to 50 percent of the mortgage. However, the second mortgages required high commissions and interest rates that were as much as double the rate of the first mortgage. Equally problematic was the term of the loans. The loans lasted only five years and then needed to be renegotiated. While the boom was in progress, the land held its value and people were able to secure a new first and second mortgage. However, as the real estate development cycle came to an end and values fell below the initial purchase price, homeowners were not able to secure financing.

The full impact of the stock market crash of 1929 hit the real estate market by 1931. Values dropped precipitously along with payrolls. The city's employers reduced wages and the number of workers so that by 1931, employment stood at only 75 percent and payrolls only 60 percent of their 1927 totals. Charities supported 170,000 families, and 40,000

These raised ranches in the Marquette Park area were the successors to the Chicago Bungalow and

helped meet the housing demand created by World War II veterans. (Photograph by Mati Maldre.)

families had "doubled up" with relatives or left Chicago, causing rents and home values to plummet by as much as 50 percent in some districts.

For the homeowner, these were tough times. The Chicago Title and Trust Company computed that the increase in foreclosures in Cook County grew from approximately 2,000 in 1926, to more than 15,000 in 1932. The banks that lent the money could not help either. Between 1930 and 1933, 163 of Chicago's 200 banks suspended operations. In most cases, the cause was linked to real estate. Lending in the Bungalow Belt in the previous decade tied up funds in houses and buildings that could not be liquidated upon foreclosure. While the more successful downtown banks could lend on real estate, they refused to tie up funds. The bungalow building boom cycle collapsed.

Chicago's Bungalow Belt is the legacy of an extraordinary real estate boom fueled by innovation, access to capital, and optimism. The solid bungalows built in the 1920s housed generations of Chicagoans, and the tightly ordered blocks provided the basis of community building. Bungalow owners became neighbors and developed communities that would celebrate patriotic, ethnic, and religious traditions, and pulled together for block parties and celebrations. Even as some of the owners struggled through the Great Depression, new owners arrived to replace the unfortunate who lost their piece of the American dream. The newcomers found the same amenities that attracted the Bungalow Belt pioneers. However, instead of watching houses grow out of the prairie, the succeeding generation of bungalow owners grew bonds that formed enduring communities. On the far fringes of the city, isolated bungalows stood for many years as testimony to the dreams of developers with poor timing. Eventually, they too would be surrounded by a new generation of housing built to meet the needs of the next group to come home from war.

four

THE BUNGALOW AND THE NEW AMERICAN WOMAN

by Jan Cigliano

Women played a crucial role in the development of the Chicago Bungalow. The purchase of a bungalow was a symbol of family pride and upward mobility. Pictured here are Vlasta (Svoboda) Shaw and her daughter, Geraldine, in front of the Shaw family bungalow in Berwyn in 1949, on the event of Geraldine's graduation from Nazareth Academy. (Courtesy of Barbara Hrbek.)

Aturn of a century beckons for definitions. It provides a neat turning point, a punctuation mark in the ongoing evolution of history—of design, culture, society, politics, the family. For the historian, the bungalow—a house type—and the *new* woman—a label—identify a nationwide phenomenon in housing during the early twentieth century. Four simultaneous factors revolutionized the American house and household living. First was house design: the bungalow prevailed after 1900. The bungalow's popularity spread nationwide, from Illinois to North Carolina, Florida, Texas, California, Washington, and elsewhere. The second factor was a doubling of the country's urban population between 1890 and 1920, which pressed demand for new, affordable housing and spread the geographic boundaries of every American city. The third factor, which is more nebulous, but equally important, was the growth of the professional middle class and its rising involvement in social and political concerns, notably the Progressive movement. The fourth was the mechanization of the home and innovations in domestic technology, including electricity, central heating, the washing machine, vacuum cleaner, and dishwasher.

Each of these phenomena informed one another. One significant result was a marked change in most women's daily lives. As the principal player in the management and caretaking of the house, the woman was effectively liberated by technological advancements; this resulted in changed responsibilities within the household and the family, and a changed role and greater involvement in social activities. Another outcome was the construction of tens of thousands of modest-sized bungalows, resulting in massive suburbanization.

The Bungalow and Arts and Crafts Movement

The Arts and Crafts Movement dominated the architectural field during the three decades between about 1900 and 1933. Among architects, high-profile designs by Frank Lloyd Wright in Chicago (the Prairie Style and Usonian design), and Greene & Greene, Bernard Maybeck, and Julia Morgan in California (Japanese- and Beaux-Arts-influenced bungalow and stick-style designs) were widely publicized in professional and popular outlets. The time was ripe for the bungalow's reception; American builders and households increasingly moved away from the larger frame of the Victorian house with its decorative shapes and complex room layouts to a more modest-sized dwelling of open rooms and efficient layouts.

As a work of architecture, the bungalow embodied the essence of the Arts and Crafts philosophy. Gustav Stickley remarked that it was "a house reduced to its simplest form where life can be carried on with the greatest amount of freedom; it never fails to harmonize with its surroundings. . . it was never expensive because it was built of local material and labor; and it was beautiful as it was planned to meet the simplest needs in the simplest way." The Arts and Crafts Movement flourished in America from about 1900 to 1930. Gustav Stickley and *The Craftsman* magazine, principal voices of the Arts and Crafts Movement, argued that modern life could be ennobled and made holy through honest, worthwhile labor. American Arts and Crafts gained a widespread following, in large part thanks to Stickley's promotion. From one city to another, Arts and Crafts societies took shape and infused the ethos of design and living into the popular conscience. The

This bungalow on 92nd and Elizabeth Street in the Brainerd neighborhood exhibits traditional Chicago Bungalow elements, including a protruding octagon bay, quality brickwork, wraparound windows, and a low-hung roof. (Photograph by Mati Maldre.)

organization of such groups as the Rhode Island School of Design, the Industrial League in Chicago, the Women's Club in Michigan, the Society of Arts and Crafts in Ohio, the Boston Arts and Crafts Society, and hundreds of others staged numerous exhibitions during this period. Among the most innovative and influential was the Chicago Arts and Crafts Society, founded in 1897 by Jane Addams of Hull House; within six months the society totaled 128 members. While Addams may be best remembered as a leading agitator for social reform, she also assumed as much importance in art reform.

URBANIZATION, SUBURBANIZATION, AND THE POPULAR BUNGALOW

Timing may well have played a central role in the bungalow's popularity. During the years that several publications showcased the architectural works and bungalow designs of Stickley, Greene & Greene, and Wright, the nation's middle class expanded exponentially.

*The Aladdin Company of Bay City, Michigan, offered this home that was typical of the standardized and precut plans for bungalows. W.J. Sovereign and Otto E. Sovereign founded the Aladdin Company in 1906. Aladdin pioneered pre-cut catalogue houses in the twentieth century. (*Aladdin Catalog, *1937.)*

Along with unprecedented economic growth, there arose a widespread desire to achieve the American ideal of homeownership. In just 20 years, 1900–1920, the number of American families who owned their own house grew by 4.7 million households—a 100 percent increase. The bungalow was the house of choice. It was affordable, modestly and efficiently sized, appropriate for middle-income lifestyles, and responsive to the growing American interest in nature. The decade of the 1920s also witnessed the most rapid rise in automobile usage; car production doubled to 4.5 million cars in a short seven-year period, 1922–1929. Mass consumption of the automobile enabled Americans to live further out from the center city, beyond mass-transit lines, thus fueling suburbanization. House building increased by unprecedented numbers, and the construction field was characterized by innovative technological innovation. "This was the great period of rationalization in American building technology," James Marston Fitch pointed out in *American Building.*

   In response to a national demand for reasonably priced, well-built, and comfortable single-family houses, architectural designs were sold inexpensively through the mail.

Mail-order (or catalog) pattern books offered complete house packages—standardized plans and pre-cut construction materials. Sears, Roebuck & Company was the market leader, followed by Montgomery Ward and the Aladdin Company, and the bungalow became the typical suburban house for millions of Americans. Indeed, the bungalow's social and economic importance stemmed from the fact that it was central to the development of the mass suburb. As Anthony King simply stated in *The Bungalow,* it "was to be the ultimate development of social and architectural trends already in motion."

The bungalow entered American culture during the 1880s and 1890s, about the same time it emerged in England. The term derived from the Hindi word *bangla,* which referred to the East Indian people who lived in low, one-story thatched huts encircled by large porches. In America, the first bungalows were simple seaside vacation cottages, a new building type, located in summer resorts along the eastern seaboard and on large lakes near the largest cities in the Midwest, South, and Northwest. On the West Coast, small, one-story Queen Anne-style cottages with breeze porches arose about the same time throughout California, mostly favored by affluent winter residents traveling from the East and Midwest to the state's temperate climate.

The bungalow house type, as a cottage or permanent home, exemplified Arts and Crafts values: simplicity, comfort, affordability, modest scale, artful form and function, natural materials, colors, forms, and environmental integration. By extension, the design was developed with a premium on efficient use of space. It was modest in overall size and scale, one or one-and-a-half stories with the second floor area under the roof structure, low to the ground in appearance with deep roof overhangs and wide eaves, a spacious front porch, rectangular or square in shape, built with natural and indigenous wood, and treated with natural and provincial colors and tones. Compared to older townhouses, in which many purchasers had lived previously, the basic difference was the emphasis on simplicity, artistry, and the open plan. As Gwendolyn Wright has pointed out, with the bungalow, the average single-family house underwent a major transformation from picturesque, irregular shapes, "to a restrained and simple dwelling, with interest focused on its scientifically-arranged kitchen." The centrally placed living room with large fireplace, linked by an open arch to the dining room, took on a symbolic function as the family room.

Importantly, a well-designed bungalow was relatively inexpensive to build, about $400–1,100. Its affordability was matched by the ease of purchasing plans and construction, whether by the homeowner or speculative builder. Historians Katherine Cole Stevenson and H. Ward Jandl have shown that building kits were as readily available in the 1910s as sewing patterns for clothes are today. George F. Barber of Knoxville, Tennessee, was the first to sell house packages in 1889. Within the decade bungalow plans were widely published in such popular magazines as *The Craftsman* (1901–1918), *Bungalow Magazine* (1909–1918), *Ladies' Home Journal*, and *House Beautiful,* as well as the handful of mail-order catalogs.

Sears Roebuck offered more than 20 bungalow models in its annual catalog, the *Book of Modern Homes and Building Plans,* first published in 1908. The female eye surely had some influence. "Each model is designed and planned by a council of experienced architects, which includes a woman," the 1929 catalog guaranteed. On the team was an interior

"She rules her domestic kingdom with woman's unerring intuition and gracious dignity. More homage to the queen of the home! The best is none to good for her."

American Builder *magazine warned developers in the 1920s not to ignore the wishes of women in designing new homes. This cartoon published in 1920 portrays the woman as "Queen of the House," and shows architects, developers, and others offering their wares to her as her children sit at her feet. (*American Builder, *August 1920.)*

design coordinator, Miss E.L. Mayer: "Every floor plan and interior decorating sketch must bear her approval before it is adopted. She must see that provision is made in the plan for pianos, davenports, radios, beds, and dressers, and all conveniences appealing to the housewife are not overlooked. She selected kitchen cupboards, the built-in ironing boards, telephone stands, and other contrivances so important in home comfort, and assists the Honor Built home builder in the selection of draperies, rugs, and other furnishings. She also suggests the most effective way of landscaping the various houses to bring out their individual charm and beauty." By 1937, female architect Aileen Anderson was on the Sears architecture team, according to a Chicago club of women architects. From its centralized warehouse, Sears sent out plans and construction manuals to homeowners and contractors by railroad. Sears profited handsomely by also offering attractive financing plans in addition to the architectural plans and materials; bungalows accounted for about half of all Sears houses built between 1908 and 1940.

There were also dozens of bungalow books available for the prospective homeowner to choose from, many originating from California. An early one was *Practical Bungalows for Town and Country* by Frederick T. Hodgson, 1906. Others included *Radford's Artistic Bungalows,* 1908, containing 200 designs; H.L. Wilson's *Bungalow Book*, 1910; and pattern books by the Standard Building Investment Company, the Building Brick Association of America, the Architectural Construction Company, Bungalowcraft, California Ready-Cut Bungalows, and others.

The bungalow's nationwide popularity also stemmed from its functionality. In Chicago, for example, tens of thousands of bungalows were built between 1905 and 1930. This was a city of middle-income families, and the growth in the metropolis took place in the outer neighborhoods beyond the core. During the period 1910 to 1916, the number of individuals living within 4 miles of State and Madison Streets in the Loop remained the same at about one million people. The number of residents in the area 4 to 7 miles out nearly tripled from 460,000 to 1.1 million people, and 7 to 10 miles out doubled from 180,000 to 332,000 residents. A large percentage of this growth was housed in newly built bungalows on the outskirts of the city. And as a rising number of second-generation immigrants were able to move out of the center city to nonurbanized or closed-in suburban areas after 1900—thanks to the aid of low-cost home mortgages through "building societies"—blue-collar workers bought their own houses, a bungalow or two-story walk-up. According to Harold Meyer and Richard Wade, with the economic prosperity of industrialization and the availability of affordable housing, "thousands of laborers emerged from the most crowded blocks into the newer, more pleasant residential streets."

THE PROGRESSIVE MOVEMENT AND A NEW PROFESSIONAL MIDDLE CLASS

At the turn of the century, the largest and most dynamic cities, including Chicago, led in economic growth and local businesses attracted young professionals. Many arrived from small towns and rural areas, feeling isolated and alienated in the dense, teaming urban

Developer William H. Brittigan built this home at 5340 West Dakin Street in the Portage Park neighborhood in 1922. It was the first house on a block that quickly developed with a mixture of bungalows and brick two-flats. (Courtesy of Anonymous Donor.)

environments. These people constituted a new middle class, among them architects, doctors, teachers, social workers, professional administrators, journalists, and economists. They encouraged one another in their respective fields and worked to improve living conditions in their cities. Some groups started as community philanthropic organizations, and advocated a cleaner, safer, more beautiful city.

"Progressivism was the central force in a revolution that fundamentally altered the structure of politics and government early in the twentieth century," observed historian Robert Wiebe. This also applied to social and architectural attitudes. Progressivism went beyond the halls of government to encompass every facet of life in the American home. In Chicago, for example, architect Allen B. Pond designed functional settlements for Jane Addams, who supported the Chicago Arts Society in the promulgation of the bungalow as the preferred house type. People like Pond found reward by applying their professional skills to humanitarian concerns and to the fledgling scientific management society of which the young professions were a part. No doubt Addams' endorsement helped the bungalow's popularity, yet the degree of influence remains unknown.

As Barry Sanders, who has studied Gustav Stickley and the Craftsmen Movement, has pointed out, popular publications, public exhibitions, and educational programs were equally instrumental in promulgating arts and crafts sensibilities. In 1896, the first issue of

This Beverly bungalow breakfast nook shows the practicality of bungalow design. As kitchens became smaller and more practical, breakfast nooks provided an easy, informal space for families to have meals without using the more formal dinning room. (Photograph by Mati Maldre.)

House Beautiful included articles and designs by proponents of arts and crafts. In 1897, Copley Hall in Boston housed the first major arts and crafts exhibition, which would give birth to the Boston Society of Arts and Crafts. Classes in manual arts appeared in high schools and colleges, which women attended—such as California Institute of Technology—as well the Rookwood Studio, Marblehead, Arequip, and Newcomb College started amateur operations and became important potteries. By 1909, Stickley was selling Craftsman furniture in 42 cities. Rural craftspeople also contributed to the interest in the arts and craft aesthetic, with small groups developing into more influential societies.

Together, the Progressive movement of women's groups, arts clubs, and professional associations represented serious advocates for Arts and Crafts ideals, including the bungalow, and took the form of a humanitarian crusade. Progressives had to organize and combine to be effective; the strength of the movement was in its association, and from the end of the nineteenth century to around 1915, Progressive societies multiplied rapidly.

Such centralized associations of women, artists, and middle-class professionals became powerful institutions and many times defeated organized businesses opposed to reform. Typical were women's clubs in many cities and counties. Women who hailed from established families and cultivated educations—Jane Addams, Florence Kelley, Lilian Wald, Sarah Decker, Katherine Edson, Josephine Goldmark, Flora Mather, Francis Boardman, Alice Woodbridge, and Mrs. Charles Russell Lowell—got the results they worked to achieve. They also advocated for important humanitarian concerns, such as well-designed and affordable housing and improved working conditions for women and children.

BUNGALOW DESIGN

"The bungalow is planned and built to meet simple needs in the simplest and most direct way," stated Gustav Stickley in 1909. It is "a house reduced to its simplest form, which never fails to harmonize with its surroundings, because its low, broad proportions and absolute lack of ornament give it a character so natural and unaffected that it seems to blend with any landscape." Because it was built of local, natural materials, he concluded, "it is beautiful." Stickley and his *Craftsman* magazine were probably the most influential voices in establishing stylistic design standards and the theoretical foundation of bungalow living. Other leading architects included Frank Lloyd Wright, who had great influence on the Chicago and Midwest areas, and Charles and Henry Greene of Pasadena, California, in the West. Throughout America's towns, cities, and states, residential architects and designers of furniture, glass, tile, textiles, and metal objects integrated their work into the bungalow environment. American families loved the bungalow's sociable front porch, leaded-glass windows, oak staircases, and wooden detailing, as well as the flexibility to alter plans to suite the individual family's size and budget.

From places as far ranging as upstate New York, the northern Midwest, California, North Carolina, Florida, Texas, Georgia, and Washington State, two-style bungalows were very common, mixing the Craftsman with the California style, Prairie with the Shingle Style, Colonial Revival with Mission Revival. The bungalow was a wonderfully flexible

This entrance to a Beverly bungalow exhibits the mixture of Art and Crafts and Prairie School elements in the brick arches, limestone insets, and planter. (Photograph by Mati Maldre.)

The HUMPHREY Radiantfire

MAKES THE FIREPLACE USEFUL AS WELL AS ORNAMENTAL

The Humphrey Radiantfire will flood the living room with *glowing, radiant heat* in one minute after lighting.
It will save firing the furnace for two months in the fall and spring.
It wil *save a ton of coal* a month in the winter time.
It can be run for two days at the cost of lighting the furnace once.
It burns ordinary City Gas, and costs approximately three cents an hour to run—using natural gas less than a cent an hour.
It will produce more heat than any other Gas Fire.
It is *absoutely and positively odorless.*
A variety of designs provide harmonious equipment for rooms of various decorative treatment and affords selection to suit the taste of your clients.

Write for special architectural catalog.

We advocate unreservedly building for permanency and the fixed connection of heaters in fireplaces where they are ready to use on cold nights, rainy days and the spring and fall before the furnace is started and then all through the winter as an auxiliary.

GENERAL GAS LIGHT COMPANY

*The General Gas Light Company promoted the Humphrey Radiantfire fireplace as a substitute for traditional hearths. While still maintaining the ideal of the fireplace as the center of home life, it proclaimed the advantages of a clean gas fire as opposed to the old-fashioned dirty wood burning fireplaces of the nineteenth century. (*American Builder, *October 1921.*)

building form that adapted to many variables—climate, technology, site, and topography.

Purists such as Stickley viewed prepackaged house kits as diluting the indigenous regionalism that, for them, was the essence of the Arts and Crafts ethos. It was true that mail-order kits largely replaced local materials and design elements with pre-cut lumber, nails, doors, and other "craftsman" parts, yet middle-income homeowners across the country made decisions based on economical living rather than intellectualized aesthetic ideals (Stickley's furniture, for example, was expensive). Indeed, Stickley's greatest influence was setting the ideal standards of bungalow design. Most families chose less expensive materials and omitted handcrafted woodwork, metalwork, and built-in furniture. Even so, one can find hundreds of historic bungalows that were "regionalized" with local wood-frame or cedar-shingle walls stained in a natural shade of brown or honey (along the West Coast and South), stucco-daubed walls and tile roofs (in the Southwest), brick walls and rolled asphalt roofing (in the Midwest), and rounded cobblestone in foundation walls and chimney stacks (in the Mid-Atlantic states).

In Chicago, developers and contractors built tens of thousands of Chicago bungalows after 1900 until about 1930, mixing Prairie-style features with Craftsman and other Arts and Crafts influences. Based on designs by Prairie School designers, the one-and-a-half story Chicago Bungalow was typically narrow across the front and longer in depth to fit the city's dense subdivision lots. Built of locally manufactured bricks, the Chicago Bungalow featured a splayed horizontal roofline, geometric art-glass motifs reminiscent of Wright's work, and internalized floor plans that protected interior spaces from the outdoors rather than opening out to it. Long and narrow floor plans arranged rooms back-to-back to minimize hallways, concentrated living areas, and contained air drafts to economize heating costs. Enclosed porches and sunrooms typically extended from the dining room or living room, at the rear or front of the house, their leaded-glass windows included geometric or floral motifs. The small entrance porch led into an enclosed vestibule and separate foyer, all designed to keep the cold Chicago air outside and to prevent drafts from flowing into the living room inside. The Prairie Style bungalow was also associated with the Chicago Bungalow and Frank Lloyd Wright.

The bungalow's comfort derived from unobstructed views and flowing circulation—principal rooms opening into each other through wide, wood-trimmed portals, such as archway, double French doors, and simple thresholds. The ground floor typically contained the major living spaces, which made it convenient to clean—living room, dining room, kitchen with pantry, two bedrooms, and one bathroom, and the full-floor attic area under a broad roof structure that could be built out as second-floor bedrooms. Interior doorways and windows were framed by easy-to-clean planar wood-stained trim and curtainless windows; compare this to Victorian high-relief moldings and draperied windows and doors. In addition to respecting Arts and Crafts aesthetics, the openness enhanced fresh-air circulation and natural light in modestly scaled houses. Only bedrooms, bathrooms, and privates studies or libraries are typically set off by a closed door, designed for privacy and covered with paint, papers, curtains and walls, trim and windows.

The bungalow floor plan, with minimal or no hallways, integrated the architecture with the interior design. Built-in furniture maximized space and enhanced the open appearance: window seats and glass-fronted cabinets in the living room, bookcases in the sitting room, a sideboard and china cabinets in the dining room, benches, cabinets, and utility closets in the kitchen, chests and closets in bedrooms and bathroom hallways. The bungalow also introduced the clever technique of using inner walls to conceal household utilities and service areas, such as stairways and closets, the ironing board and breadboard, leaving outer walls free for large windows.

The living room was the bungalow's largest room, evoking warmth, comfort, and openness. At the center of the open floor plan, the living room set the stylistic theme for other rooms, whether rustic, informal, or elegant. Sitting nooks, often integrated in the room's inglenooks were cozy spaces. They might also be separate rooms, such as a library. Individual chairs and small sofas accommodated reading and talking among family members, rather than contemporary living rooms furnished with couches, easy chairs, and coffee tables for lounging and group entertaining. The living room centered on the fireplace, which could be seen as a maternal expression of hospitality with family and friends. Henry Saylor's popular 1911 pattern book, *Bungalows: Their Design, Construction and Furnishing,* preached that the fireplace is the symbolic center of the house: "a bungalow without a fireplace" is like "a garden without flowers."

The dining room, an extension of the living room, was crafted to achieve the ambience of domesticity and elegance and was typically the most formal room—an ensemble of architecture (French doors, sliding pocket doors, stained wood trim, ceiling beams, wall paneling, and high-paneled wainscoting, painted or papered walls), built-in furniture (naturally stained sideboards, window seats and glass-doored cabinets, plate rail), and moveable furniture (table, chairs, sideboards, china, pottery, textiles). In many bungalows, the dining room opened into a sunroom of wood-trimmed windows and summer screens on all sides.

Architects designed bedrooms to be bright, cheerful, and well ventilated—intended as a restful and quiet place. They were separated from public living areas by a private hall or located in a secluded area of the house, often on the second floor. The typical 1910s–1920s design placed the principal two to three bedrooms on the ground floor, adjacent to or adjoining the one full bathroom. This was an efficient layout that minimized hallways and made morning clean-up (bed and bath) easy and efficient. Sited to receive morning sun and natural light throughout the day, the bedroom was a moderately spacious room with operable windows designed for fresh-air ventilation and cross-circulation and closets vented with fresh-air shafts to the roof. Walls covered with a light-toned or muted paint or paper—ideally white or ivory enamel—enhanced brightness and illumination. A minimal décor of light and washable fabrics and simply crafted furniture created a fresh and sanitary environment. Furnishings, including bed, bed stand, low dresser with wall mirror, and perhaps a sitting chair and small desk were selected for their function rather than their ornamental appeal.

The bungalow bathroom exhibited the same cleanliness, freshness, and brightness as the kitchen and bedroom. It was finished in white or ivory porcelain with nickel-plated fixtures. Walls of white rectangular ceramic tile and enameled, creamy white-painted pearled woodwork were designed for easy cleaning. The high-paneled or high-tiled wainscot wall, at three-quarters or half height, was bordered at the top by a narrow cornice or tiles laid horizontally. (Colored ceramic tiles arrived in the American bathroom in the 1920s, often as an accent band.) Designed in proximity to the bedroom, (and typically adjoining it) the bathroom accommodated the individual's well being in a fresh, airy, and quiet environment. Second-floor bedroom and bathrooms were more common in Chicago Bungalows, designed for a colder climate, which filled out the floor area under the roof structure rather than splaying out across the land.

The bungalow bathroom generally contained cast-iron fixtures finished in porcelain—the toilet, hot and cold running water in the pedestal sink, the clawfoot bathtub, the standing shower, and the embedded wall medicine cabinet, a carry over from the Victorian area when mechanized bathrooms first appeared. Built-in linen and toiletry cabinets framed the bathroom or adjacent bathroom-bedroom hallway. Simplicity guided the craftsmanship in the bathroom, including plainly milled oak or mahogany trim, built-in cabinetry, and porcelain-tile floor. One or two small operable windows brought in light and air

MECHANIZATION OF THE HOME

The impact of technology—electricity, the elevator, the automobile—on early twentieth-century American life was enormous and changed the basic structure of daily life—for the American woman and the family. Advances in technology along well-established lines of endeavor as well as quantitative increases in the volume of production characterized the period. For 100 years before, clothes were washed and dried by hand, food was canned and baked in the household kitchen, the floor and carpet were cleaned by sweeping, the room was lighted by oil or gas, and the house was heated by oil or kerosene room heaters. All this changed in a period of 10 years with the widespread availability after 1900 of electricity and the innovation and distribution of the vacuum cleaner, running hot and cold water, the mechanized washing machine and clothes dryer, the electric light, iron, refrigerator, and central coal heating.

Technology greatly influenced the design of the bungalow, as can be seen in the work of George C. Elmslie, a protégé of Louis Sullivan. Electricity, most of all, allowed the single-family house to become smaller in scale and more efficient in plan. In the kitchen, the innovation of the cooking range, the oven, the percolator, and the refrigerator reduced floor-space requirements throughout the house. The central heating system, vacuum cleaner, washing machine, and sewing machine made cleaning easier and less time-consuming. In addition, the telephone enabled immediate communication to shops, which made storage space less important; stocks stayed on grocery shelves rather than in the house closet. Such activities as bread making and food canning moved out of the house. The smaller dwelling with fewer rooms was more functional and popular.

There is historical precedent for such evolutionary trends. Historian Eric Hobsbawm documents the significance of "invented traditions" throughout time, from ancient to modern cultures. Indeed, "invented traditions," such as the mechanized bungalow, linked the seamless flow of life and history from year to year and century to century. "Invented traditions," he said, were traditions that were constructed and formally instituted,

This photograph from the American Builder *lauds the development of the vacuum cleaner. In this case the vacuum is used to clean a radiator, another symbol of the modern house.* (American Builder, *January 1921.*)

traditions that emerged in a less traceable manner and in a brief and dateable period and established themselves rapidly. The bungalow came to popularity within the context of the Arts and Crafts tradition, a tradition that is traceable to and continuous with the past. At the same time, the *new* woman, who was liberated from household drudgery by technological invention, introduced new values and norms of behavior to household design and living. In this we have "invented tradition," which was continuous with the past and also responded to a new and novel set of situations.

The mechanized kitchen, a tremendously important innovation, had the biggest impact on the daily lives of women. It emerged during the bungalow's heyday as domestic servants became less common in the American household. Efficiency experts claimed that the time for a more efficient kitchen was none too soon. Mrs. Christine Frederick, one authority, wrote in "The Servantless Home," a series of *American Builder* magazine articles, "As I have often laughingly said, no architect who ever planned a kitchen would ever wash dishes in it himself for a single week without going on strike!" Mrs. Frederick and others

McCRAY
REFRIGERATORS *for* ALL PURPOSES

for Residences

FOR GROCERS

FOR HOTELS, CLUBS
RESTAURANTS, HOSPITALS,
INSTITUTIONS, ETC.

FOR FLORISTS

FOR MEAT MARKETS

FOR DELICATESSEN STORES

McCRAY Refrigerators give economical, dependable service. This is why architects specify them for the finest hotels, clubs, institutions and residences.

Investigate the McCray Refrigerator and you, too, will realize why architects and the public have accepted the name McCray as a guarantee of satisfaction.

Use has proven that the patented McCray cooling system insures a constant circulation of cold, dry air throughout every compartment—insuring perfect food preservation. *McCray not only carries a large variety of refrigerators in stock for prompt shipment, but builds them to order in any desired style or size for all purposes.* The outside icing arrangement is a McCray feature, very desirable and convenient for residences.

FREE PLANS. The ideas and suggestions of our draftsmen are at your service—simply send us a rough sketch showing the general outline of your client's refrigerator requirements. We will gladly send blue prints and draw up specifications.

Get Our New Catalogs for Your Files.

No. 95 for Residences
No. 53 for Hotels, Clubs and Restaurants
No. 64 for Meat Markets
No. 72 for Grocers and Delicatessen Stores
No. 75 for Florists

McCRAY REFRIGERATOR CO.
3160 LAKE ST., KENDALLVILLE, INDIANA
Salesrooms in All Principal Cities

*As part of the "electrical" revolution in household consumer goods, refrigerators began to make their impact on middle-class homes in the 1920s, replacing the older iceboxes. (*American Builder, *March 1922.)*

claimed that in the average kitchen, "the woman must dance backward and forward, across and about before she can serve a meal. . . she must go from closet to door, through and across and back." New, efficient kitchen design "routed" work between the sink, stove, and table. There was to be no wasted space in high, out-of-reach closets. Spaces were to be smaller and compact, with more built-in furniture. It furthered healthful, sanitary design by introducing stove hoods to funnel cooking smoke, draft coolers for perishable food storage (refrigerators by contemporary standards), built-in flour bins and breadboards, and built-in storage cabinets as part of the bungalow's architecture. Built-in wooden cabinets, cupboards, and drawers expressed the linear lines of wooden carpentry, and plain white or ivory enamel painted walls offered maximum washability and brightness in natural light. Windows above the sink and counter area produced a cheery work environment and increase the spacious feeling.

The kitchen was the exclusive domain of females, whether "housewives" or "maids." Before electricity and running water, most of their waking hours were spent here. Electric

*Architects designed the compact bungalow kitchen with efficiency and sanitation in mind. Notice the built-in ironing board and the breakfast nook designed for convenience and cleanliness. (*American Builder, *January 1922.)*

*Wash Day was removed from the kitchen to the basement in the modern bungalow. Electricity again came to the aid of the housewife with the development of the washing machine. (*American Builder, *March 1921.)*

appliances appeared in bungalows after 1920, and the greatest rationalization of space in bungalow design occurred in the kitchen. Servants disappeared from domestic service when industrial labor shortages made working outside the home more financially attractive. There was also the "progressive" rejection of the master-servant household. Because the majority of household tasks were performed in the kitchen, "every step saved there save untold energy through a lifetime of occupation in domestic duties." In the ideal design, everything folded away in a "pocket" space—ironing board, linen dryer, folding table, kitchen cabinet, and breakfast nook. Fittings for the bungalow kitchen, wrote W.T. Comstock in *Bungalows,* should be "as condensed as the equipment of a yacht."

The bungalow kitchen was a small, efficient, separate space, designed to ensure cleanliness in food preparation and containment of unappealing sights and odors. No space was to be wasted. Convenient cupboards, air cooler, and work table combined to enhance culinary duties. "To many a housewife," wrote Gustav Stickley in *Craftsman Bungalows*, "a study of the kitchen will prove interesting. This room is finished in white enamel, and is most convenient in arrangement of built-in features. There are numerous cabinets and drawers, the usual sink, a hood for the range, a draught cooler, a built-in flour bin, a disappearing bread board, and an ironing board that folds up into its own special cabinet." He concluded, "The kitchen is equipped with all modern conveniences, so that the work of the housewife is more of a pleasure than a drudgery."

Kitchen design respected bungalow ideals of efficiency, healthfulness, and brightness while it incorporated innovative technologies. Such values as simplicity in design and detail were evident in undecorated and unornamented surfaces, with cabinets painted white or ivory enamel and floors of white or white-and-black ceramic tiles, sanded pine, or light-toned linoleum ensured ease in washing and cleanliness in cooking. This design created the most healthful work environment. An efficient space plan designed to save steps and make housework more pleasant incorporated the full complement of conveniences that mechanization provided: sanitary plumbing, running water, hot air furnaces with automatic controls, hot water, steam plants, and built-in furniture such as cabinets and counters, the kitchenette and wall refrigerator, compact pantries, and dishwashing machines. Smaller than the Victorian-era kitchen, the bungalow kitchen featured space-saving built-ins rather than freestanding tables and armoires.

So significant was the mechanization of the home and the evolving role of the woman in it that *American Builder* published a year-long series during 1920–1921 on "Woman and the Home." The first exclaimed, "Electricity her Servant," thanks to the innovation of electrical, laborsaving appliances. A photograph caption for a California bungalow cited the personal and familial benefits, "Beautiful, Modern Homes Are Cornerstones of Happy Families and Housewives. Builders Owe to Themselves and Humankind to Make Homes as Convenient and Drudgeless as Possible. The Contractor Who Built This Delightful Home for Dorothy Phillips, Charming Screen Actress, Has Undoubtedly Succeed in Making It a Real Home. Look at the Smile!" The emphasis on easing the workload for women and the resulting improvement in human welfare was boastful but also a believable claim at that time. Electricity provided enormous ease to household life specifically and American living generally.

In the servantless house—the norm after 1890—the woman washed, ironed, cleaned,

While electric washing machines may have helped lighten women's workloads, the backyards of the Bungalow Belt remained important places for hanging the wash, as can be seen in this Portage Park photograph taken in the 1940s. (Courtesy of Anonymous Donor.)

cooked, and sewed. Electricity reduced the duration and endurance involved in these activities, from the washboard and hand wringer to the electric washer, from the fire-heated iron and brick to the electric iron, from the hot and smoky wood-burning stove to the electric range and fireless cooker, from backyard water wells and dishwashing at every meal to the electric dishwasher once a day. "The Pleasure Expressed in the Faces of These Women Is Ample Evidence of the Progress of Modern Building Equipment!" Even the sewing machine reduced the physical treachery of household work. *The American Builder* cited a revealing statistic, "Almost any woman can treadle a machine for 200 stitches a minute. A very strong woman can do 400 stitches. . . . When she harnesses electricity to her needle she can do 1,500 stitches a minute and hold it as long as necessary."

The electrical wiring system was as new to house design as was the electrical appliance. Flexibility became the watchword. More and more outlets were required where they had been unnecessary only five or ten years before in a modestly wired house. By 1921, the *American Builder* recommended 25 outlets per home, an average of 2.5 per room.

95

Bungalow architects and builders scaled the house modestly and gave intelligent attention to the arrangement and size of rooms. "The construction of the home is no longer exclusively a man's job because the woman very often is the source of new ideas," the *American Builder* editor Grace T. Hadley reported. "She is a firm believer in modern appliances because they have become her stock in trade." Women after 1920 became more involved in house design, which covered the interior trim, the location of equipment, the finish of floors, and the arrangement and size of rooms. It was the greater involvement of women in domestic management that most influenced the efficient house plan. "The growth of woman's sphere has effected vital building principles," architect William B. Reedy wrote in the *American Builder* article, "Building 'Drudgeless' Homes." As women's roles in domestic affairs became more prominent, female input on house design became more relevant. Women had the time and energy to become more active in politics, civic affairs, and social movements because of mechanization. Women's public involvement provided a stronger voice and platform for women in the house and in society. As such, women gradually assumed a more prominent position in household management and in consulting with the house builder. The *American Builder* concluded, "Nowhere is the modern emancipation of woman more clearly shown than in the home. . . . The transition has been one of amazing speed and extent. And in this development, electricity, modern building, space-saving devices, and labor-saving appliances have played a big part." The woman's role—in the household, in social affairs, and in house design—changed with the introduction of laborsaving technology. As a result, the inter-relationship of architectural design, household technology, the woman's changed role, and the influence of community and political groups changed the structure of domestic life in the early decades of twentieth century. The bungalow symbolizes this change.

This classic octagon bungalow on the 9700 block of South Seeley was built in 1926 for approximately $9,000 and exhibits typical Chicago Bungalow features, including a small front porch and octagon sunroom attached to the living room. Mayor Richard M. Daley announced the Historic Chicago Bungalow Initiative on the front lawn in September 2000. (Photograph by Mati Maldre.)

This octagon bungalow in the Beverly neighborhood has very strong horizontal lines emphasized by the limestone bands above and below the windows and by the broad overhanging roof. The narrow, casement windows are balanced by the horizontal window panels above. (Photograph by Mati Maldre.)

Generous windows facing the street bring the outdoors into the house, and the side entrance portico gives the residents a place to be outside and yet be sheltered. This house in Marquette Park has a broad overhanging roof to provide shade and double-hung windows that open at the both the top and bottom to create circulation keeping the bungalow cool in the summer. (Photograph by Mati Maldre.)

This row of stucco and cedar bungalows stands on the 9800 block of South Walden Parkway, near the tracks of the Rock Island District of the Metra commuter line in the Beverly neighborhood. They contain the same basic floor plans and lot placement as brick Chicago-style bungalows while using different materials. Access to transportation and bungalow development went hand in hand. (Photograph by Mati Maldre.)

This west suburban Berwyn block contains a mixture of stucco and brick bungalows. The stucco bungalow contains an open front porch and has some characteristics of its California cousin but is much narrower because it sits on a typical Chicago area lot. For more than 80 years, bungalows have represented the fulfillment of the American Dream to hundreds of thousands of residents. (Photograph by Mati Maldre.)

J.L. Koster designed this large Oak Park bungalow on Rosell Avenue for William J. McKenzie in 1930. Larger than most Chicago bungalows, it includes a side drive and a two-car garage. Notice the tiled pagoda-style roof and the use of limestone inserts. (Photograph by Mati Maldre.)

Built in 1930 at 99th and Hamilton, this large bungalow designed by Lyman J. Allison includes a tile roof, prominent octagon bay, and arched windows. The pitch of the roof is sharper than that of the typical bungalow. (Photograph by Mati Maldre.)

This bungalow on Albion Street in West Rogers Park provides a striking example of tile work, brickwork, and limestone inserts, including the window columns. (Photograph by Mati Maldre.)

Bungalows are often criticized for their lack of uniqueness, but examples from all over the city and suburbs, including this one featuring a Swiss Chalet roof from the 4500 block of North Sacramento, attest to the diversity of their design. (Photograph by Mati Maldre.)

A "bungaloid" mansion sits prominently on the corner of 66th and Troy Streets in the Marquette Park neighborhood. It dominates the neighborhood around it. Developers often reserved corner lots for larger more stately bungalows. In this case, the building was built beyond typical bungalow characteristics while maintaining many bungalow design elements and combining them with others, including Greco-Roman columns, an open porch, and turrets. (Photograph by Mati Maldre.)

This "bungaloid" mansion on West Hollywood Avenue in West Rogers Park pushes the definition of bungalow to its limits while still maintaining features common to less spectacular bungalow-type homes. (Photograph by Mati Maldre.)

Two Czech-American brothers built these twin "jumbo" bungalows with parallel driveways on Riverside Drive in suburban Berwyn. The homes symbolize the upward mobility and suburbanization of this important Chicago-area ethnic group. Notice the intricate terra cotta details and columns, tile roofs, as well as the extensive use of face brick. (Photograph by Mati Maldre.)

Despite the characterization of uniformity, diverse styles appeared throughout the Bungalow Belt. Appearing in this photograph of 58th Court in Cicero are a Chicago Bungalow, a less typical bungalow with a unique roofline, and an apartment building. (Photograph by Mati Maldre.)

The Beverly bungalow basement window shown here includes limestone inserts to highlight the brickwork and create various design elements. The attention to detail that went into the living room windows was duplicated in these basement windows. (Photograph by Mati Maldre.)

Terra cotta surrounds and accents these bungalow windows on South Damen Avenue, showing a fine example of the type of detail and workmanship available to bungalow owners. (Photograph by Mati Maldre.)

This Berwyn bungalow features intricate brickwork and leaded Prairie-Style windows. The builders created interest with the use of arches over the entryway, windows, and ramparts to contrast with the strong horizontal lines. (Photograph by Mati Maldre.)

These intricate leaded Prairie-Style glass windows are located on the side of this stately suburban Berwyn bungalow. Notice the fine detail and the gold mirror design. Construction of the curved face of the bay was more expensive than flat, octagonal fronts and required more skilled masons. (Photograph by Mati Maldre.)

The beamed ceilings, fireplace, French doors, wraparound windows, and extensive use of simple yet beautiful woodwork give beauty to this Morgan Park Arts and Crafts home. (Photograph by Mati Maldre.)

The Gregory House is a large Andersonville bungalow that has undergone extensive restoration and is now operated as a bed and breakfast. The wraparound windows of the front octagonal bay and the customary bungalow fireplace give a simultaneous sense of openness and coziness to this home. (Photograph by Mati Maldre.)

Chicago Bungalows included an open floor plan allowing for efficient use of space as seen in this view of the Gregory House. Arched openings tied the various public rooms together. Bedrooms often stood off of the main rooms and were connected by a small hallway. (Photograph by Mati Maldre.)

Architect Nels Brick designed this wooden bungalow on Bryn Mawr Avenue in Andersonville in 1914. Notice the wide kitchen windows and the relationship of the kitchen to the dining and living rooms. (Photograph by Mati Maldre.)

The bungalow has proven to be a very versatile housing form. A variety of ethnic groups have made them their own through interior and exterior decoration and landscaping. This bungalow backyard on the 10100 block of South Bell exhibits the Latino roots of the Jirasek-Arias family. Pottery, decorations, and paints imported from Mexico, along with a high fence recreate an urban Mexican private space. (Photograph by Mati Maldre.)

This West Rogers Park landmark home was built by Fred Winters in 1928. While not following typical Chicago Bungalow details, it incorporates most of the basic ideas of the form, including a front bay and wraparound windows. (Photograph by Mati Maldre.)

Bungalows are notable for their ability to withstand Chicago's fierce winters. (Photograph by Mati Maldre.)

These bungalow-style two-flats on the 7100 block of South Washtenaw in the Marquette Park community show how the bungalow style could be stretched beyond the concept of the single-family home. Each level of these buildings reflects the basic bungalow floor plan. They also include attics and basements. Many families preferred to purchase two-flats in order to defray the costs of ownership or to provide housing for extended families. (Photograph by Mati Maldre.)

five

IT'S MORE THAN A BUNGALOW
PORTAGE PARK AND THE
MAKING OF THE BUNGALOW BELT

by Ellen Skerrett

The Dettmers family celebrated the Fourth of July on the front lawn of their Norwood Park bungalow in 1925. (Courtesy of Bill Tyre.)

The Bungalow Belt neighborhoods that emerged in Chicago between World War I and the Great Depression not only changed the city's landscape, they provided a model of community that has endured for generations. First and foremost, the bungalow neighborhood embodied the American dream of homeownership for thousands of working-class Chicagoans. To move from a densely populated area of frame tenements heated by coal or wood-burning stoves to a street lined with bungalows constituted a high point in the lives of ordinary families. The contrast between the old neighborhood and the new was profound—the bungalow featured a modern tile bathroom, kitchen, living and dining room, bedrooms with closets, ventilated basement, back porch, and an attic that could be remodeled into more bedrooms as the family grew. It also had a front lawn and backyard.

For women and children, the bungalow held special appeal. Without domestic help, the task of running a household was daunting, but mothers of small children found that the layout of the bungalow and its yard freed them from "the need of constant supervision." Unlike rural areas where homes tended to be far apart, city blocks often included 36 bungalows separated by narrow "gangways," passages extending from the front of the house to the backyard. Sidewalks were another distinguishing feature of the Bungalow Belt, square after square of pavement that linked homes to one another. In addition to promoting neighborliness, these ribbons of concrete provided boys and girls with hard surfaces on which to ride bikes, roller skate, pull wagons, draw with chalk, and play hopscotch, marbles, and jacks. With dozens and dozens of children on each block, the front stoops and streets of the Bungalow Belt were filled with activity from early morning until late at night, and few families could remain strangers for long. Little wonder that these neighborhoods are remembered so fondly by so many!

Crucial to the success of the Bungalow Belt was the network of institutions that shaped day-to-day life—the parks, schools, and churches that gave each neighborhood its distinctive sense of identity and place. These were landmarks in every sense of the word, structures that extended the ideals of the "City Beautiful" movement to the local level where ordinary people lived. Paradoxically, while bungalow neighborhoods proved immensely popular to Chicagoans of diverse ethnic and racial backgrounds, the sentiment was not universally shared by urban planners who tended to regard them as "monotonous," row upon row of modest brick dwellings in a "sea of uniformity." In 1913, for example, the prestigious Chicago Club sponsored a national competition to design a residential neighborhood on 160 acres of a "typical quarter section of land in the outskirts of Chicago." Considering the miles of vacant land in urban areas, Progressive reformers believed that planners and real estate developers had a unique opportunity to "intelligently direct and control the growth of cities." But what should these new neighborhoods look like?

CONCEPTS OF THE IDEAL COMMUNITY

Not surprisingly, most of the entries submitted for the City Club competition abandoned Chicago's distinctive grid system of streets at right angles. Architects preferred the curving streets and open green spaces advanced by proponents of the Garden City movement in England or by the diagonal streets popularized by Daniel H. Burnham in his "City Beautiful" plans for Chicago, Washington, D.C., and San Francisco. The jury awarded Wilhelm Bernhard first place. It praised his "striking architectural plan" for housing 1,280 families in single family dwellings and flats so "well adapted to the Northwest side of the city." Key elements of the winning design included a Prairie-style elevated railroad station intended to decrease automobile traffic—already a growing problem in urban areas—and a village square surrounded by public buildings and businesses that were strictly separated from residences. The jury applauded Bernhard for designing a private park in nearly every residential block. These open spaces would provide "safe playgrounds for the children and encourage a neighborly spirit among the families in the block." The fact that Bernhard planned to decrease lot size from 25 feet (the prevailing Chicago standard) to 20 feet did not trouble the jury since it believed that grouping houses would "avoid the monotony which. . . a straight line of single houses offers."

At the time of the 1913 competition, Chicago's "prairies" were being transformed, almost overnight, into urban neighborhoods of modern brick apartment buildings and single-family homes, many of them bungalows. Although the real estate sections of city newspapers bore witness to this revolution in the housing industry, architectural journals and national magazines paid scant attention. Invariably, they characterized one-story bungalows as ideal homes for the middle classes who sought escape from the noise and dirt of the city in suburbs where children could reclaim their birthright—"green grass and bowering trees. . . woods and flowers. . . air and freedom." Yet as Hugh J. Fixmer's entry for the City Club competition demonstrated, workers of modest means also aspired to freestanding homes "with open spaces for flowers, garden, and recreation."

Fixmer, a civil engineer with the Chicago Bureau of Street Engineering, knew from experience that the city's grid system promoted, rather than retarded, neighborhood development and community. Since 1905, he had worked with the Board of Local Improvements, an agency that widened many of the city's oldest streets and replaced wooden sidewalks with concrete pavement. Fixmer claimed that his design was an "engineering rather than an architectural solution to the housing problem," and he made no apology that it was "more practical than esthetic." His plan placed apartments and businesses along streetcar lines and separated pedestrian traffic from vehicle traffic as a way to achieve "quietness, cleanliness, and exclusiveness without loss of democratic character." Fixmer also paid particular attention to the needs of children, locating the schools, churches, theater, park, library, and social center all within walking distance for the 1,270 families in the neighborhood. In fact, he was convinced that "such surroundings, conveniences, and attractions" would foster real home life and contribute to the physical, moral, spiritual, social, and intellectual well-being of American children. He argued simply that, "A home once established here is permanent, for the property cannot be used satisfactorily for any other purpose."

In his "aesthetic review" of the 1913 City Club Competition, architect Albert Kelsey singled out Fixmer's plan as bereft of "graceful and attractive city-making," and predicted that it would "delight sordid real estate operators and be heartily approved by the average matter-of-fact city engineer." But for thousands of Chicagoans, such criticism missed the

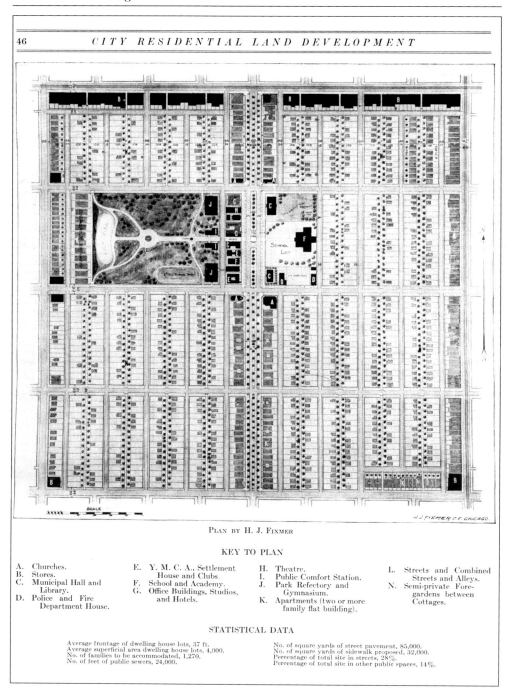

PLAN BY H. J. FIXMER

KEY TO PLAN

A. Churches.
B. Stores.
C. Municipal Hall and Library.
D. Police and Fire Department House.

E. Y. M. C. A., Settlement House and Clubs.
F. School and Academy.
G. Office Buildings, Studios, and Hotels.

H. Theatre.
I. Public Comfort Station.
J. Park Refectory and Gymnasium.
K. Apartments (two or more family flat building).

L. Streets and Combined Streets and Alleys.
N. Semi-private Fore-gardens between Cottages.

STATISTICAL DATA

Average frontage of dwelling house lots, 37 ft.
Average superficial area dwelling house lots, 4,000.
No. of families to be accommodated, 1,270.
No. of feet of public sewers, 24,000.

No. of square yards of street pavement, 85,000.
No. of square yards of sidewalk proposed, 32,000.
Percentage of total site in streets, 28%.
Percentage of total site in other public spaces, 14%.

Chicago Engineer Hugh J. Fixmer's entry for the 1913 model neighborhood competition was sponsored by the City Club of Chicago. (From City Residential Land Development, *1916.)*

mark. Far from regarding the new Bungalow Belt neighborhoods as "compact monotony," residents took pride in the appearance of modern homes that shared a common design and materials, and they welcomed the opportunity to live in close proximity on streets with such amenities as curbs and sidewalks. Equally significant, thousands of men, women, and children enjoyed the benefits of the "City Beautiful" movement through their local parks, schools, and churches. A case in point is the Portage Park neighborhood on Chicago's Northwest Side.

PORTAGE PARK: THE PARK

In 1910, less than 6,000 people lived in the Portage Park area, roughly bounded by Lawrence Avenue (4800) on the north, Belmont Avenue (3200) on the south, Narragansett Avenue (6400) on the west, and Cicero Avenue (4800) on the east. Originally part of Jefferson Township, Portage Park began to experience commercial and residential development after the extension of the Milwaukee Avenue streetcar line in 1906. But it was the creation of a 36-acre park at Irving Park Road and Central Avenue that put the neighborhood on the map. Developers Arthur W. Dickinson and George F. Koester took the lead in creating a park district for the area west of Cicero Avenue and persuaded residents to name it "Portage," after the trail used by Pottawattomie Indians to carry their canoes overland from the Desplaines River to the North Branch of the Chicago River.

Both Dickinson and Koester were familiar with the success of the "small parks" movement led by reformers at Hull House, the pioneering settlement Jane Addams and Ellen Gates Starr established in 1889. The campaign to provide parks in congested immigrant districts began in 1893, with the opening of the Hull House Playground on Polk Street, just east of Halsted. By 1904, there were nine more playgrounds in the city with an annual attendance of nearly three-quarters of a million people. As a result, "the corner gangs, through the influence of playgrounds, have become the athletic gangs of the neighborhood."

Although Chicago enjoyed a long history of park development, its famous necklace of greenery—Lincoln, Washington, Jackson, Humboldt, Garfield, and Douglas Parks—had failed to keep pace with the city's growth. Architect Dwight Perkins called on city dwellers "to act again for Chicago with a faith similar to that shown by [nineteenth-century civic boosters]." In a Labor Day speech on September 5, 1904, Henry G. Foreman, president of the South Park Commissioners, discussed Chicago's commitment to providing recreation facilities for its citizens. In reviewing the tremendous progress made by the Small Parks Commission, Foreman noted that 14 parks were being created on the South Side alone, each with its own fieldhouse containing gymnasiums for men and women as well as meeting rooms for clubs and branches of the Chicago Public Library. Reminding his audience that "there is a crying necessity for useful as well as ornamental parks," Foreman reported that 90,000 men, women, and children had used the new swimming pool in McKinley Park in its first season.

Chicago's small parks quickly achieved a national reputation. In June 1907, delegates from more than 30 cities traveled to Chicago to participate in the first conference of the Playground Association of America, heeding President Theodore Roosevelt's call to see "one of the most notable civic achievements of any American city." In her best-selling book, *The Spirit of Youth and the City Streets*, Jane Addams recalled her pleasure at watching hundreds of children playing games and the "bright colored garments of Italians, Lithuanians, Norwegians, and a dozen other nationalities [who danced] for the pleasure of the more stolid Americans." While Progressive reformers promoted the goals of the small parks movement, Myron West responded by organizing the American Park Builders Company in 1911. As the former general superintendent of Chicago's Lincoln Park, West had played a key role in building fieldhouses on the North Side. He understood the public demand for bathing beaches and facilities and traveled outside Chicago preaching the gospel of parks and playgrounds in creating the "City Beautiful." In addition to praising West's handsome brochure on American parks, the national journal *Parks and Cemetery* noted that his company was prepared "to undertake the actual work of park and landscape construction."

West soon had a client close to home; in 1912, the Portage Park Commissioners hired him to design a new park along Irving Park Road. This was a unique opportunity to combine athletic facilities and landscaped grounds. Reflecting the "modern tendency in playground development," West included a baseball field, children's play area, and a lagoon with four interconnected lakes. Not only did his design ensure that Portage Park would be an oasis in the midst of a city neighborhood, but it underscored the central role children would play in the life of the Bungalow Belt.

While the small parks movement was concentrated in immigrant Chicago neighborhoods, its effects were felt across the nation. In preparing a *Handbook of City Planning* for the general public as well as architects, urban planner John Nolen asserted that "Every city worthy of the name has public parks of some sort, and they are now recognized as a necessity of city life, just as streets and water and schools are a necessity." He argued that "they contribute to the pleasure and health of urban populations more than any other recreative feature, and furnish the most necessary and valuable antidote to the artificiality, confusion, and feverishness of city life." To J. Horace MacFarland, Chicago's small parks provided outstanding examples of "civic pride and provision." Easily accessible for children on foot, these "country clubs. . . of the people," with their schedule of organized activities and sports successfully competed with "hundreds of saloons, dance-halls and worse."

The formal opening of Portage Park on July 4, 1913, set the tone for neighborhood events for years to come. Unabashedly American, the ceremony featured a "parade in the morning by members of fraternal organizations. . . and a children's parade." Throughout the 1920s, the annual "old fashioned Fourth of July" celebrations—complete with fireworks—attracted crowds of 40,000 to the area, including prospective home buyers. To the sons and daughters of immigrants who had grown up in densely populated neighborhoods near the Chicago River, the broad expanse of Portage Park offered opportunities generally available only to the city's elite who lived near Lake Michigan. R. Morgan Barngrover, attorney for the park district, urged commissioners to raise funds for an outdoor pool as "a good substitute for lake bathing," and to provide suitable landscaping that could "take the place of river and lake views and beaches."

The Portage Park pool, c. 1930s, was replaced in 1959 by an Olympic-sized facility, site of the 1972 Olympic Swim Trials. (Courtesy of Chicago Park District.)

The sand-bottomed lagoon in Portage Park that opened in 1916 was an immediate hit, drawing men, women, and especially children. While families still made regular trips to the new Municipal Pier off Grand Avenue and to Clarendon Beach on the lakefront, the neighborhood pool provided instant relief from Chicago's muggy weather. Years later, Barngrover characterized the Portage Park swimming pool as "one of the most attractive features of the district," and he pointed to the history of the park as confirmation that: "open space ultimately becomes the most precious thing in a city."

From the outset, Portage Park functioned as a community center, bringing together new residents of the Bungalow Belt—no small feat considering their diverse ethnic and religious backgrounds. In addition to native-born whites of Anglo Saxon descent, the neighborhood included a high percentage of first and second generation Swedes and Germans. Many of the adults had moved from older industrial neighborhoods near the Chicago River where trees—much less parks—were few and far between. Little wonder that proximity to Portage Park was so highly prized and that it drove up real estate prices on the surrounding blocks. Much more than simply an open space in the midst of new brick bungalows and two flats, the park embodied the Progressive reformers' faith in the power of play and recreation to form American citizens. The first Memorial Day celebration in Portage Park on May 31, 1920, provides a classic illustration.

Since the Civil War, Chicagoans had traditionally observed Decoration Day with pilgrimages to cemeteries where they laid wreaths on the graves of veterans and listened to patriotic speeches. By the time World War I ended, however, ceremonies were held in parks. But more than the setting had changed. No longer spectators, children took an active role in the celebrations. For example, students from three public schools in the neighborhood gathered on the great lawn of Portage Park and participated in the flag-raising ceremony, parade, calisthenics, military drills, and exercises. But what made Memorial Day so memorable for 400 boys—and girls—was the elaborate schedule of races, 19 in all, featuring the broad jump, relay, and the 25-, 50-, and 60-yard dash.

To meet the growing demand for sports facilities, Portage Park Commissioners hired Clarence Hatzfeld to design a fieldhouse (1922) and a gymnasium (1928). Hatzfeld (1873–1943), a Chicago native, had begun his career as a draftsman for Julius H. Huber, whose family firm helped to rebuild the city after the Great Fire of 1871. As a member of the Chicago Architectural Club, Hatzfeld was influenced by the work of Dwight Perkins, one of the city's most highly respected Prairie School architects. He eventually shared office space with Perkins and between 1912 and 1921, the firm of Hatzfeld and Knox designed Prairie and Craftsman-style bungalows in the Villa neighborhood just east of Portage Park.

As the most prolific designer of fieldhouses in Chicago parks, Hatzfeld generally favored Tudor Revival styles, but in Portage Park he created two distinctly Prairie-style structures of variegated brown-green pressed brick. The fieldhouse and gymnasium commanded prominent sites in the park, blending in well with the brick two-flats and bungalows that lined neighboring streets.

A survey compiled after Portage Park was consolidated with the Chicago Park District in 1934 singled out the gym/natatorium as "a fine building whose main entrance is reached by a series of three elevations. The middle section is used frequently as a bandstand. The assembly hall has a capacity of one hundred and fifty, while the entire building with pool can accommodate one thousand."

Beyond contributing to the impressive body of Prairie School architecture in the Midwest, Portage Park's fieldhouse and gym represented a new concept in park development, what noted landscape architect Frederick Law Olmsted (1870–1957) of Boston called "Recreation Centers." In an address at the nineteenth national conference on city planning in 1927, Olmsted, son of the designer of Chicago's Jackson Park and New York's Central Park, claimed that Chicago had pioneered the idea of public recreation facilities "more extensively and systematically than in any other city." In addition to offering indoor and outdoor sports, neighborhood parks extended the work of social settlements such as Hull House by providing children with "a great variety of interesting, healthful activities. . . artistic, dramatic, and social." But, Olmsted warned, in order to duplicate the success of the Chicago movement, planners needed to follow certain guidelines. He noted that while public transportation tended to increase the service area for adults, a distance of more than half a mile from the park posed a serious problem. In a "walking city" such as Chicago, experience had shown that "broad bands of railroads,

Clarence Hatzfeld's Prairie-School design for the Portage Park gymnasium featured a curving stairway and four brick lanterns with green tile roofs. (Courtesy of Chicago Park District.)

unbroken stretches of industrial property, and rivers or lakes constitute[d] very definite limits" to park development. Likewise, business streets could adversely affect parks because they tended "to mark off the boundaries of neighborhoods and of gang kingdoms."

To children coming of age in the 1920s and 1930s, Portage Park was a central institution in their lives. Located just a short walk from all corners of the neighborhood, it was "the largest and most completely equipped park on the far northwest side." Consolidation with the Chicago Park District brought further improvements, both physical and social. According to the first annual report issued by the unified park system in 1935, new cinder drives were built in Portage Park, 22 acres of lawn were reconditioned, 900 shrubs and 24 Chinese elms were planted, more than 100 panes of broken glass were repaired, a new chlorinating machine was installed in the natatorium, and the baseball fields were reopened. At the height of the Depression, few urban—or suburban—parks could equal its schedule of activities: "archery ranges, baseball and football diamonds, picnic grounds, tennis courts, softball and volleyball areas, a toboggan slide, a wading pool, children's playground, and every other considerable advantage dear to the heart of the amateur sports enthusiast."

PORTAGE PARK: THE SCHOOLS

While neighborhood parks and playgrounds became a centerpiece of the Progressive movement in Chicago, reformers also devoted much attention to enlarging the role of public schools. Once again, Hull House led the way. At the turn of the century, Jane Addams and Ellen Gates Starr supported efforts to open public schools for evening classes and lectures, especially in immigrant districts. But the idea of schools as social centers also gained new currency in Bungalow Belt neighborhoods such as Portage Park where the public schools were the largest, and often the most expensive, structures. The increasing visibility of the Chicago Public Schools was due in great measure to the work of Dwight Heald Perkins. A native of Memphis, Tennessee, Perkins was educated in the Chicago Public Schools and studied at the Massachusetts Institute of Technology. He returned to Chicago in 1888 to work for Daniel H. Burnham, subsequently chief of construction for the World's Fair of 1893.

In addition to his private practice, Perkins was a civic leader in the movement to create small parks and in 1905, he became chief architect for the Chicago Board of Education. During his five-year tenure, he supervised the construction of nearly 40 schools and new additions throughout the city. According to architectural critic Peter B. Wight, the new structures reflected a radical departure from conventional designs. Instead of "pilastered walls, terra cotta Renaissance capitals and galvanized iron cornices," Perkins designed fireproof schools using "brick and stone or brick and terra-cotta, each in its right place as a constructive material fulfilling the purposes as planned." Many of the new grammar schools, for example, were three stories in height, with high-ceilinged classrooms, gymnasiums, and assembly halls with stages suitable for dramatic productions or "lantern" lectures. Perhaps the most famous Perkins' design was for Carl Schurz High School at Addison Street and Milwaukee Avenue. Prominently featured in the Chicago Architectural Club's 1908 annual exhibition, the Prairie-style school received favorable mention in such journals as *The Brickbuilder,* and it quickly became a landmark on the Northwest Side.

That the new Chicago Public Schools represented an unprecedented investment in the city became abundantly clear in 1910, when board president Alfred R. Urion charged Perkins with "incompetency, extravagance, and insubordination." At issue in the highly publicized trial was the cost of alleged "frills" such as assembly halls in new buildings when many schools had to operate on double shifts. Despite doubts about the cost of new public schools, Superintendent Ella Flagg Young defended Perkins' emphasis on artistic construction. She recalled that, "when I first went to the Normal School as superintendent I expressed my dissatisfaction with the fact that so much money had been expended to beautify the entrance when so many children had no seats, but when I saw the influence on the young people of the beauty of that marble corridor I changed my mind and approved the expense."

The Ole A. Thorp School, designed by Arthur Hussander and completed in 1918, extended the ideals of the "City Beautiful" movement to Chicago's public schools. (Courtesy of BauerLatoza Studio.)

Nowhere was the need for new public schools more apparent than in Portage Park. As a result of the construction of hundreds of bungalows and two-flats, the neighborhood's population increased to 25,000 in 1920, and by 1930 it numbered 65,000. Within a decade, three new schools opened their doors, all designed by Arthur F. Hussander: Gray (1911), Portage Park (1915), and Thorp (1918). Hussander succeeded Perkins as chief architect of the Board of Education and continued his legacy of monumental school building. Of the five new structures he superintended, the O.A. Thorp was among the most elaborate. Despite building restrictions and shortages of coal during World War I, the three-story school was completed by June 1918, at a cost of $350,000. Its 32 classrooms with a seating capacity of 1,600 made it one of the largest in the city, and its auditorium and gymnasium ensured that the Thorp School would "meet the growing needs for community activities."

Civic reformers believed that public schools had a unique opportunity to function as community centers, bringing together the young and the old for educational programs that provided "a finishing touch to the work of citizen-making." As early as 1913, Jane Addams had decried the fact that city schools "opened for educational purposes only five hours a day for five days a week." Writing in the *Ladies' Home Journal*, she observed that "our forty-million-dollar plant in Chicago is used only thirteen hundred hours a year, while the people, by whom the schools were built, find their recreation outside as best they may." Republican mayoral candidate William Hale Thompson campaigned on the issue and after election day in 1915, kept his promise to establish community centers. Within two years, 45 Chicago schools opened their doors in the evening for a period of 23 weeks. The response from Chicagoans was overwhelmingly positive, and school officials soon noticed that "excessively large attendance" occurred on nights that featured gymnastics, dancing, and moving pictures rather than "public welfare meetings, lectures and general social meetings."

Fittingly, the Ole A. Thorp School in Portage Park was named after a former chairman of the building and grounds committee of the Chicago Board of Education who believed that public schools contributed to Chicago's reputation as "the greatest city in the world." At the time Thorp died in 1906, Progressive reformers had made great gains in providing playgrounds near schools in congested neighborhoods. Charles Mulford Robinson, a national authority on city planning, drew on the Chicago experience, noting that "the movement for municipal playgrounds has resulted in the use and increased appreciation of school yards and the demand that henceforth all public schools shall have yards." But he warned that: "until the playground has beauty, the good deed falls short of the perfection it ought to have." Thanks to the foresight of civic leaders such as Ole Thorp, Chicago's neighborhood schools featured "garden plots, increased play ground facilities, and opportunities for school yard decorations with trees, shrubs, and flowering plants."

PORTAGE PARK: THE CHURCHES

Progressive reformers spoke and wrote passionately about parks and public schools as agents of Americanization. Yet religious institutions also played a crucial—if unacknowledged—role in transforming the children of immigrants into citizens. From the 1830s on, families from Germany, Ireland, Bohemia, Poland, Italy, and Russia had invested scarce resources in constructing churches and synagogues that became the center of their community life as well as visible landmarks in Chicago. These edifices represented an enormous financial investment on the part of working-class families, much to the chagrin of social reformers who believed that funds could be better spent on reformatories and workhouses for the poor.

It took decades to complete and decorate a permanent house of worship, much less to pay off the mortgage. But in congregation after congregation, the story was the same: the never-ending fundraising efforts—bazaars, concerts, picnics, raffles, and door-to-door collections—helped to create community. Moreover, the results were often spectacular. German Lutherans, Catholics, and Jews, for example, hired well-known Chicago architects to design edifices that compared favorably with the elegant churches built by transplanted New England Yankees and Kentuckians. Irish, Polish, Bohemian, Italian, and Lithuanian immigrants were also enthusiastic supporters of "brick and mortar" Catholicism, building massive Gothic and Romanesque churches whose steeples vied with smokestacks in industrial neighborhoods near the Chicago River. For hundreds of thousands of immigrants, the experience of creating a church or synagogue through voluntary contributions was an important first step in becoming American. Although the committees that purchased property and sought clergy tended to be predominantly male, women played a critical role in fundraising efforts. They also took particular delight in casting their ballots—at 10¢ a try—in popular voting contests. Years before they received the franchise, working-class Chicago women voted "early and often" in church bazaars, raising money for stained glass windows, pews, statues, paintings, and other marks of refinement.

Overlooked by city planners was the role religious congregations played in developing modern urban neighborhoods. In a version of "chain migration," houses of worship and parochial schools in the emerging Bungalow Belt often attracted families who had lived near each other in the old neighborhood. For many families with deep attachments to a particular church or synagogue, the move to a new residential district could be difficult because it meant severing connections with a beloved place. However, the opportunity to create something new also appealed to the children and grandchildren of immigrants who were constructing a future for themselves as Americans. Beyond providing much-needed work for skilled artisans and architects, churches enjoyed a special status. However modest in scale and design, congregations regarded them as "built for the ages," intended to outlast the most ornate neighborhood bank or movie theater.

Swedish Lutherans were the first of several ethnic groups to put their imprint on the Portage Park neighborhood. In 1893, they purchased 80 acres of land south of Irving Park Road between Central and Austin Avenues for the Martin Luther College subdivision.

THE CHURCH AND PARSONAGE

Nebo Lutheran Church, home to generations of Swedish Lutherans, is now the Portage Park Center for the Arts. (Courtesy of Jennifer La Civita Kimbrough.)

But the area was still too remote for many Swedes, and the school relocated to Rock Island, Illinois (now home of Augustana College). The dream, however, persisted and in 1901, Rev. A.S. Sandahl began organizing Nebo Swedish Evangelical Lutheran Church, with a congregation of 42 adults and 24 children. The following year, members built a small frame church for $1,600, a substantial sum considering the size of the congregation. Thanks in great measure to the bungalow-building boom, membership soared to nearly 300 by 1912, enough to warrant the construction of a substantial brick edifice at the southwest corner of Dakin Street and Menard Avenue.

Amidst all the war news from Europe, the official dedication of Nebo Lutheran Church on February 14, 1915, was cause for celebration and the congregation turned out in force for the event. According to a history of the church, the $27,751.13 price tag did not include "the amounts paid by the Ladies' Aid, the Young Peoples' Society, and different individuals for carpets, altar, pulpit, piano, candelabra, etc."

For generations of Swedes in Portage Park, Nebo Lutheran remained a place of great beauty in their lives and in their neighborhood. Church publications reveal the dramatic impact of the Bungalow Boom: the Sunday School class grew from 12 students in 1902 to

PROGRAM

3 - Act Operetta
"PICKLES"

Given by the

NEBO LUTHERAN CHURCH
CHOIRS

in the

O. A. THORP SCHOOL

on

December 10th and 11th, 1936

•

Sponsored by the

O. A. THORP
PARENT - TEACHER ASSOCIATION

PRINTED BY THOMPSON & ZIMMERMANN, CHICAGO

In the midst of the Great Depression, the choirs of Nebo Church entertained community residents in the auditorium of the Thorp School. (Courtesy of Jennifer La Civita Kimbrough.)

400 by 1922, and children accounted for nearly one-third of the congregation's 410 members. When the church decided to raise $20,000 in May 1922 to liquidate its debt, a committee solicited donations from local businessmen. Reflecting the amicable relations between neighbors of different ethnic and religious backgrounds, the publicity book included ads for local grocers, doctors, undertakers, bakers, barbers, jewelers, tailors, and automobile dealers, as well as subdividers such as Albert J. Schorsch and homebuilders Lundquist & Nelson. The campaign paid dividends; in addition to reducing the church debt, the congregation was able to redecorate the interior, purchase a pipe organ, provide seating for the choir, pave the alley, and landscape the grounds. While justifiably proud of the role Nebo Lutheran played in the growth of the Portage Park neighborhood, members were also aware of the significant changes that had occurred within their congregation as they wrestled with the question of Americanization. The transition from Swedish to English that began in the Sunday School in 1906 was completed by 1920, and the issue was resolved without "any controversy."

Like their Swedish Lutheran neighbors, Catholics who moved to Portage Park also used their churches as a way to create identity and community. One of the major differences,

In advertising his subdivision of bungalows in 1917, Albert J. Schorsch emphasized its location within walking distance of Portage Park, the Thorp School, the Irving Park streetcar line, as well as "stores and all churches." (From The Schorsch Family Centenary, *October 22, 1995. Courtesy of Dr. Albert J. Schorsch, III.)*

REAL ESTATE—Northwest Side.

$20 a Month Buys This Bungalow

In a beautiful subdivision a block from cars; near new million dollar school, 40-acre park, stores and all churches.

NOW IS THE TIME TO BUY.

Our modern homes, brick or frame, have not yet advanced in price and when sold cannot again be duplicated.

Also 2-family homes for sale on rental basis.

TAKE IRVING PARK BLVD. CARS TO 60TH AV.

A. J. SCHORSCH
6001 IRVING PARK BLVD.

however, was that all English-speaking Catholic parishes organized after 1900 had clearly defined boundaries. Families who moved into a new neighborhood could no longer return to their old parishes for baptisms, marriages, or funerals but were required to attend the church closest to their home. The Catholic policy, as Protestant church planners recognized, had important consequences. According to Victor E. Marriott of the Chicago Congregational Union, Catholic churches in Chicago "march across the map in regular array with almost equal spacing in parishes while the Protestant Churches are bunched like berries in certain spots, [leaving] great empty spaces where there are no Protestant churches."

That Catholic parish development kept pace with the growth of the city was no accident. Archbishop James E. Quigley, who headed the Chicago diocese from 1902 until 1916, believed that "a parish should be of such a size that the pastor can know personally every man, woman, and child in it." Our Lady of Victory Church in Portage Park, established in 1906, was one of scores of "mile-square" parishes established throughout

The bungalow of Elizabeth and Albert Schorsch at the corner of Meade Avenue and Dakin Street, c. 1920s, featured ornamental brick, stained glass windows, and a Prairie-Style tile roof. (From The Schorsch Family Centenary, *October 22, 1995. Courtesy of Dr. Albert J. Schorsch, III.)*

CLASS OF 1931

Much of the growth of St. Pascal parish was due to the parochial school, established in 1916. At the time the class of 1931 graduated, the new church was nearing completion. (Courtesy of St. Pascal School.)

Chicago. Located near the Milwaukee Avenue streetcar line, the parish attracted "Catholic families of the inner city, who are anxious to get away from the smoke and congestion and who wish to give their children a beautiful home, near a parochial school and church." The new combination brick church and school structure, dedicated in 1911 at 4444 North Laramie Avenue, blended in well with the neighborhood's bungalows and two-flats, and provided plenty of "growing space" for the new congregation. However, by 1914, the need for a second parish west of Central Avenue between Belmont and Lawrence Avenues was clear.

St. Pascal's provides a stunning example of the way in which a parish put down roots in the Bungalow Belt and contributed to the development of the larger neighborhood. Pioneer parishioners attended Mass in the "nickel show" on Irving Park Road east of Narragansett, and remembered with amusement how Catholic children who returned for the movie on Sunday afternoon would forget and "genuflect before taking their seats"! By 1916, Rev. George Heimsath had directed the construction of a church and school building at 4242 North Austin Avenue but the lack of sidewalks was a problem for children and adults alike. The offer of 4 acres of property on Irving Park Road by real estate developer Albert J. Schorsch in 1921 proved to be a turning point in the history of the parish. Relocating on a major thoroughfare not only put the church "in the middle of

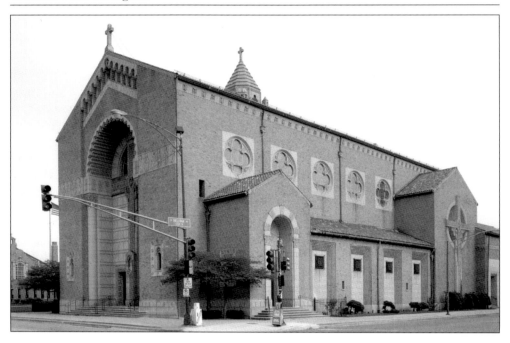

St. Pascal Church, designed by Chicago architects Bartholomew Hotton and Raymond Gregori, was built by local craftsmen during the height of the Great Depression. Its Spanish Mission-style exterior includes ornate terra cotta ornament. (Photograph by Mati Maldre.)

the parish," but it established St. Pascal's as a focal point of the Portage Park neighborhood.

Beginning in 1917 and continuing through 1927, the Schorsch Brothers created the Irving Park Boulevard Gardens subdivision of nearly 1,000 bungalows on what had been a truck farm. Ads for the brick homes, which ran in the German language press as well as in Chicago daily papers, stressed proximity to the streetcar line on Irving Park Road, schools, and churches.

As an immigrant himself, Albert J. Schorsch understood the hopes and aspirations that men and women harbored for their American-born children. Born in Austria-Hungary in 1888, Schorsch had emigrated with his parents and six siblings in 1895. The family settled in Morris, Illinois, where Albert found work as a night watchman in a bank. After taking a correspondence course, he landed a job as a mail sorter, first on a railway car and later at the main Chicago Post Office. Albert attended college at night, but his plan to become a dentist was cut short by the death of his father in 1913. Before long, he convinced his entire family to move to the Northwest Side of Chicago, where he had begun selling real estate with a co-worker from the post office. In business for himself by 1917, Albert was able to hire several of his brothers who provided "in-house concrete work, carpentry, masonry and painting."

The success of these immigrant entrepreneurs was not limited to bungalows. In 1927, the Schorsch firm built the Patio Theater building at the northwest corner of Irving Park

114

Boulevard and Austin Avenue, and in 1928, the elegant West Irving State Bank directly across the street.

In the spirit of Daniel Burnham, members of St. Pascal's made "No Little Plans." Despite the fact that the parish numbered only 400 families in 1924, the congregation embarked on an ambitious building campaign, constructing a Mission-style combination structure of yellow brick that included classrooms, church, and auditorium with stage.

Even after the Depression struck in 1929, there was no stopping; on May 10, 1930, the *Chicago Daily News* reported that work would begin soon on a $200,000 church with a seating capacity of 1,500. A distinctive feature, according to architects Bartholomew J. Hotton and Raymond J. Gregori, was the 47-foot cross on the front elevation. With its red tile roof, 150-foot tower, and terra cotta trimmings, St. Pascal was the tallest—and most ornate—church in the Portage Park neighborhood, rivaling the nearby Patio theater, which residents nicknamed the "Spanish shrine of silent art."

At the same time that businessmen were transforming "Six Corners" into one of the city's largest regional shopping districts, men and women continued to reinvest in their community by financing new churches, schools, and auditoriums. Members of Messiah Lutheran, for example, followed the lead of German Lutheran and Catholic congregations in building a combination church and school (with parsonage upstairs) in 1926. Surrounded by brick bungalows, the structure at 6200 West Patterson Avenue continued to serve as the primary worship space for the next 23 years. And on the eve of the Great Depression, the neighborhood's oldest congregation, Jefferson Park Congregational, began a new chapter in its history by hiring the sons of Norwegian immigrants, Christian Michaelsen and Sigurd Rognstad, to design a Colonial-style church at 4733 North London Avenue. Although city planners and architectural critics took little notice of the ecclesiastical building boom that transformed the landscape of the Bungalow Belt, residents needed no reminder that churches made a difference in the fabric of urban life. Despite diverse ethnic and religious backgrounds, they knew from personal experience the truth of the old nursery rhyme: "Here is the church, here is the steeple, open the doors and see all the people."

The parks, schools, and churches created in Bungalow Belt neighborhoods such as Portage Park constituted a significant, if unappreciated, legacy of the "City Beautiful Movement." Often unknown outside their immediate locale, they nevertheless became cherished landmarks, as important in their own right as Chicago's more famous buildings. Although invisible in the literature on city planning until recent years, the Bungalow Belt neighborhoods constructed between 1914 and the Great Depression have been rediscovered by architects and residents alike. Once dismissed as examples of "monotonous regularity. . . [reminiscent] of soldiers on parade," the homes and institutions that contributed to the Bungalow Belts' distinctive sense of place are now being studied and celebrated.

Hugh Fixmer would be pleased. Although he lost the City Club competition in 1913, his plan bore a remarkable resemblance to the bungalow neighborhoods that subsequently were built throughout the city. Against the conventional wisdom of the day, Fixmer insisted that Chicago's distinctive grid offered benefits to children and adults alike because they could reach all parts of the neighborhood quickly and safely—on foot. And while few homeowners could afford the 60-foot lots that he believed were ideal, generations of Bungalow Belt residents have enjoyed the cement sidewalks "bordered and shaded by magnificent trees," as well as the alleys at the rear of their homes. Moreover, after nearly 90 years, urban planners and civic leaders have come to understand that houses alone cannot guarantee "a fuller community life," but are inextricably linked with public and private institutions—schools, parks, churches, and transportation. In the end, Hugh Fixmer's design for a Chicago neighborhood was a winner.

six

MOVING ON UP
CHICAGO'S BUNGALOWS
AND THE AMERICAN DREAM

by Dominic A. Pacyga

Charles S. Lee developed the 3700 Block of West 62nd Street in 1927. He purchased the land from the Hines Lumber Company for $100,000 and erected 60 bungalows with a frontage of 1,800 feet on 62nd Street and 62nd Place between Lawndale and Central Park Avenue for a total cost of $450,000. This bungalow block sits just to the west of St. Nicholas of Tolentine Catholic Church. Parishioners dedicated the English Gothic-style church building in 1939, after 15 years of planning and raising funds. (Photograph by Mati Maldre.)

In 1927, Father James F. Green, the pastor and founder of St. Rita of Cascia Catholic Church, remarked that only a handful of Catholic families lived in the area when the Augustinian Friars arrived to establish their presence on the prairie on Chicago's Southwest Side. "There were seven families in the parish when I first came here (1905), three widows with children, one widow with no children, and three regular families." Father Green took up temporary residence at St. Anne's Church in Englewood to the east, which already had a large Catholic, mostly Irish and German American, population. Within 20 years, St. Rita's Parish, straddling the Gage Park and Marquette Park neighborhoods, grew to be one of the city's more prosperous parishes as Catholics moved in large numbers to the area leaving behind older immigrant and working-class neighborhoods. The Irish in particular made St. Rita's home. The parish, in turn, spawned several other Roman Catholic parishes across the Southwest Side, including St. Clare of Montefalco, St. Nicholas of Tolentine, St. Gall, and St. Adrian parishes. Green founded St. Rita College (High School) and organized a parochial grammar school. The years after World War I saw the rapid expansion of the parish as bungalows appeared up and down neighborhood streets. In 1930, St. Rita of Cascia parish numbered 6,000 families, and 1,400 children attended the parochial school. By the time Father Green died in 1936, his life's work had firmly established white ethnic Catholic communities across the city's Southwest Side. Catholics arrived at the same time that the Chicago Bungalow appeared. The appearance of both Catholics and bungalows seemed to be part of the same process.

So did the arrival of the automobile. In 1913, Henry Ford began assembly line production of the Model-T. The Chicago Bungalow emerged after 1915, as a modern housing form on the edge of the city's built-up neighborhoods. The car, the bungalow, and new neighborhoods catering to an emerging ethnic middle class seemed to be all part of the same phenomenon. The American dream of a single-family detached home seemed more and more within the reach of skilled blue-collar workers and the emerging white-collar class. Apartment dwellers looked to the prairie on the outskirts of the city to fulfill their dreams of owning a home and of living in a more "modern" and even more American neighborhood. In the 1920s, the city grew quickly at its edges. Thus was born Chicago's Bungalow Belt.

THE GROWTH OF THE BUNGALOW BELT

Situated in a band around the city, the Bungalow Belt grew on land left over from the land boom of the 1890s. For over 20 years, this land lay fallow in one-time suburbs such as Chicago Lawn, Beverly, Austin, West Rogers Park, and Jefferson Park. The city had swallowed much of this land in the great annexation of 1889, and added other neighborhoods later. Land developers looked to these areas as Chicago's traction companies expanded streetcar and elevated service to the city's edges. The combined impact of better public transportation and the automobile along with reasonably cheap land values set the stage for residential expansion. So did the dreams, aspirations, and even fears and prejudices of Chicago's expanding white middle and lower middle-classes. The move to the Bungalow Belt meant upward mobility, and in some cases flight from newer ethnic and racial groups making their way into Chicago's industrial workforce. In either case, the population on the edges of the city expanded rapidly in the years after 1910.

In the 1920s, Gage Park, a community just to the southwest of the Stock Yard District, saw its population more than double to 31,535 residents. Its neighbor to the south, Chicago Lawn, witnessed a growth of more than 300 percent to 47,462 inhabitants. West Elsdon, West Lawn, and Clearing to the west of Gage Park and Chicago Lawn also saw construction during this era, although not to the same extent as their neighbors. Both Clearing and West Lawn benefited from the opening of Municipal (Midway) Airport in 1926. The same story of expansion and housing development played its way out on the Northwest Side of the city. Portage Park's population jumped from 24,439 in 1920, to 64,203 ten years later. Jefferson Park's population exploded from 5,825 in 1920, to 20,532 in 1930. Norwood Park's residential numbers grew from fewer than 3,000 in 1920, to over 14,000 on the eve of the Great Depression. Austin on the city's western edge also took part in the real estate boom of the 1920s. Originally a small village in the Township of Cicero, Austin joined Chicago in 1899, following a bitter battle over the extension of the Lake Street Elevated Railroad. It soon grew into a Chicago neighborhood. Austin's future was tied to the growth of public transportation. The opening of the Division Street streetcar line in 1915 spurred the development of North Austin. The community's population had reached more than 74,000 by 1920, but the Bungalow Boom increased the number of residents to more than 131,000. The housing market exploded all across Chicago as developers built bungalows, apartment buildings, and commercial structures at the city's edges.

CHICAGO LAWN AND THE BUNGALOW BELT

In the mid-1920s, Southwest Side businessmen with roots in Chicago Lawn's various neighborhoods began to publish a newspaper, the *Liberty Bell,* to promote the district and the entire Southwest Side. Like other local newspaper ventures, the *Liberty Bell* called for more investment in the neighborhoods it served and petitioned for better public transportation, police and fire protection, and schools, while lauding the area as a good investment. The newspaper served the area southwest of the intersection of West 55th Street and Western Avenue to the city limits, the newly emerging Southwest Side Bungalow Belt. Its end of the year listing of local improvements in 1926 pointed both to the increased residential investment in the area and to local hopes for the future.

Transportation emerged as an important theme in this listing of accomplishments. Henry Hehl of the Gage Park Improvement Association announced that 10 additional trailer cars would be added to the Western Avenue streetcar line. The Marquette Park Improvement Association took steps to have bus service extended west on Marquette Road. In response, the Chicago Motor Coach Company announced the extension of services on Marquette Road as far west as Kedzie Avenue in August. Meanwhile, assurances were made by the city that West 63rd Street would be paved west to the city limits. The newspaper noted that in May the city had announced plans to pave Cicero Avenue. The following month, the Chicago Surface Lines had made known plans to spend $250,000 for new trolley tracks and to create a permanent roadbed on West 63rd Street from Hamlin Street to Cicero Avenue. In December 1926, 200 people met at a Methodist church on 50th and Lincoln (Wolcott) in the Back of the Yards neighborhood to present a petition for the opening of 55th Street west of the Baltimore & Ohio Railroad tracks. Two thousand residents signed the petition. People from Back of the Yards were moving south and west into Gage Park, and they wanted the thoroughfares open for development. Also in 1926, the Grand Trunk Railroad announced that plans to elevate its line cutting through the area would cost $10,000. The railroad also established better service on its suburban commuter line, which stopped on 63rd Street and Central Park Avenue in Chicago Lawn.

The *Liberty Bell* proclaimed 1926 as the most prosperous year in the district's history. Developers erected nearly $20 million worth of new buildings on the Southwest Side that year, resulting in more than 1,500 new structures. Of these, 1,092 were residential buildings worth over $6 million. The spring and summer of 1926 had seen a great increase in construction. In 1927, the Southwest Side's 15th Ward had a population of 103,395 residents among its many neighborhoods, an increase of 69 percent in six years. This made it the fourth most populous ward in the city. Most of this growth occurred in the area to the southwest of 55th and Western Avenue. In addition to the Bungalow Boom

Chicago's outlying neighborhoods depended on commuter trains to connect them to downtown. Pictured here in 1890, the Chicago Lawn Station provided a focus for the neighborhood developed by James Webb and John Eberhart. (Courtesy of Chicago Lawn Historical Society.)

transforming local neighborhoods, four public schools opened in 1926, attesting to the fantastic growth of the area's school age population. These joined the four new schools that had opened the previous year. Even so, the newspaper complained of crowded schools as local class sizes continued to grow in 1926. Roman Catholics celebrated the visit of Cardinal Mundelein in May to dedicate the new St. Rita College (High School) building.

The district enjoyed the construction of all kinds of new public works. New sidewalks, sewers, and paved streets appeared. On December 18, the new Chicago Lawn Police Station opened, after many delays, on 63rd Street. The *Liberty Bell* proclaimed the new facility as the last word in police stations. The newspapers announced that, ". . . the police are quite proud of it from Capt. Paul A. Wheeler to Genevieve, the later whose duties will be to keep it just as spick and span as it was in its shininess and newness when the Lawn coppers walked in Saturday and took possession of their new home." Earlier in November, the city announced the construction of a new firehouse at 60th and Western Avenue.

Businesses also prospered in Chicago Lawn in the late 1920s. In August 1926, the new Colony Theater opened on 59th and Kedzie Avenue. West 63rd Street provided a home for many businesses, including Weiss Brothers Groceries and Meats, the Manor Radio

Chicago Lawn firemen pose in front of their fire station at 6041 South Western Avenue in 1938. City services such as police and fire protection were crucial for the development of the Bungalow Belt in the 1920s. (Courtesy of Chicago Lawn Historical Society.)

The Chicago Public Library opened the Chicago Lawn Branch Library in this ornate beaux-arts structure on the northwest corner of 62nd Place and Kedzie Avenue on March 1, 1929. Notice the

large number of automobiles parked along the busy arterial street in the early 1940s. (Courtesy of Chicago Lawn Historical Society.)

Shoppe, and the Chicago Lawn State Bank. In February 1927, Woolworth's announced the signing of a 15-year lease for one of its stores at 3108 West 63rd Street. That year, Sears, Roebuck & Company also announced the building of a large store on Western Avenue. Sixty-third Street west from Western Avenue to Kedzie developed quickly as an important shopping strip despite its relative nearness to the massive shopping district just to the east at the intersection of 63rd and Halsted Streets in Englewood.

The growth of automobile-related businesses in Chicago Lawn was especially interesting. In March of 1926, J.E. Faget announced the construction of a new $165,000 garage at 65th and Western Avenue for his Buick dealership. He predicted it to be the forerunner of an expanded motor row on the avenue. Various automobile dealerships already called Western Avenue home, including Marquette Motor Sales (Chrysler), Becker Motor Company (Ford), and Vizgard Motor Sales (Jordan Cars). The Dixie Highway Gas Station joined the Western Avenue auto dealers on October 29, 1927. Crowds attended the grand opening of the station at 60th and Western Avenue, which was jammed with customers from morning to evening. The car owners took advantage of the

The intersection of 79th and Ashland Avenue was typical of Bungalow Belt neighborhood shopping strips. Retail and entertainment districts developed wherever two streetcar lines intersected. (Courtesy of Special Collections and Preservation Division, Chicago Public Library.)

special deal offered by proprietor J.O. O'Connor of a free gallon of lubricating oil with every 5 gallons of gasoline purchased. Across the street operated the Cunningham Auto Laundry, a car wash.

A smaller automobile row developed on Kedzie Avenue where the Balzekas salesroom was located at 6010 South Kedzie. Stanley Balzekas came to Kedzie Avenue in 1921 and sold Hupmobiles, but switched to Gardner cars in 1927. Balzekas, a Lithuanian immigrant, came to the United States in 1912, and worked as a machinist and later a butcher. Within nine years of his arrival in America, he was already a prominent businessman. In many ways, his career seemed to symbolize the growth and optimism of the Bungalow Belt and of the immigrant groups attracted to it. Other car dealerships also located on South Kedzie in Chicago Lawn. Manor Motor Sales at 6443 South Kedzie sold Chandler Autos, while Robins Motor Sales did business at 6323–29 South Kedzie Avenue. Obviously the Bungalow Belt was closely connected to the spread of the automobile.

The expansion of the car culture brought dangers as well as economic benefits. Chicago Lawn had been a relatively quiet and sleepy neighborhood before the arrival of the automobile and the bungalow. Streets were not well equipped to handle the new traffic. By the late 1920s, residents asked for more streetlights and especially for new traffic lights. Armin Zapf, a local resident, pointed out that the intersections of 59th, 60th, and 63rd along Kedzie were unsafe. He stated, "It is dangerous for little tots to have to cross these streets even though they have the protection of a policeman most of the time." Progress had its price.

Class, Ethnicity, and Religion and the Southwest Side

Religious congregations also grew in the 1920s, coming to the area or building newer structures. Early Chicago Lawn had been a predominantly Protestant community. Developers James Webb and John Eberhart acquired land near 63rd and Central Park Avenue in 1876, and began what they hoped would be a prosperous, model community. By the 1920s, German Lutherans began to move into the area from older industrial neighborhoods such as Bridgeport, Back of the Yards, and Englewood to the north and east. In 1922, 12 Lutheran families organized the Nazareth Lutheran Church. Five years later, the congregation numbered over 600 and decided to build a new structure designed by architect Herbert Brand at the site of the original chapel at 60th and Spaulding at a cost of $85,000. Rev. Herbert Kohn touched on the spirit of the new Bungalow Belt when he urged churches to show the same enthusiasm that a salesman has when he ". . . goes out for his business and it will find its neighborhood full of prospects. Systematic canvassing of the community is just as useful to the church as it is to the real estate man." Another Lutheran congregation, the Evangelical Lutheran Church of the Good Shepard, was established in 1927 at 62nd and Kostner in West Lawn. That same fall yet another Lutheran congregation, Calvary Lutheran, announced a campaign to erect a $75,000 parish house at 62nd and Kenneth, also in West Lawn. Protestants continued to see the Chicago Lawn, Gage Park, and West Lawn areas as attractive residential neighborhoods. In November 1927, the Brighton Park Masonic Lodge announced it was leaving its old location near 38th and Western and was relocating to the Chicago Lawn Masonic Lodge

Bartlett Realty sponsored this hot air balloon in a Marquette Park balloon race about 1912 to advertise the Bartlett real estate development in Chicago Lawn. (Courtesy of Chicago Lawn Historical Society.)

at 62nd and Homan. The *Liberty Bell* reported that the action of the lodge resulted from the population trends of the 1920s. The paper claimed that Brighton Park had been a high-class residential district 20 years earlier, but that now a largely foreign population inhabited it. As a result, lodge members had moved farther south and now so did their institution. Indeed Brighton Park's population was becoming much more foreign born with large numbers of Catholic Poles and Lithuanians moving into the area. Native white Protestants in turn left and sought out homes in the new bungalow neighborhoods south of 51st Street.

If they had come to Chicago Lawn and Gage Park to escape Catholics and newer immigrants, they made a mistake. Although some attempt had been made to control growth in Gage Park and in the Marquette Park neighborhood of Chicago Lawn, including the refusal of large landowner Hetty Green to open her property to development, Catholics and immigrant Catholics in particular looked to the Southwest Side for the fulfillment of their particular version of the American dream. The battle between Hetty Green and Father James Green of St. Rita parish took on almost mythical proportions for the community. In 1877, multimillionaire real estate speculator, Hetty

Green had taken possession of the Gage estate from the heirs of George W. Gage, who had owned much of the land south and west of 55th Street and Western Avenue. She held on to the land and refused to develop it until 1911, when she sold the property to the Bartlett Realty Company. Father Green claimed to have influenced city hall to raise taxes on the property forcing Hetty Green to sell.

Father Green saw further problems arise once the territory, officially known as Marquette Manor but often simply called Marquette Park, began to develop. He complained that various "shark" companies soon arrived in the neighborhood to speculate on land. The Augustinian priest pointed out that crooked building companies attempted to take advantage of widows and others. Father Green further voiced distaste for the bungalow, asserting that what his parish really needed was apartment buildings. St. Rita's pastor warned that only higher population densities could provide for businesses on 63rd Street. He most probably also feared that the relatively low densities of the Bungalow Belt would hinder his plans for the development of Catholic institutions on the Southwest Sides. Certainly the wealthy parishes to the east enjoyed greater population concentrations. Nevertheless, for those Catholics arriving in Chicago Lawn, the bungalow was an attraction and they did not see it as a hindrance to either community building or economic development.

The real estate business brought developers and buyers together, and in some cases provided an opportunity for newer immigrants to try their hand at being independent businessmen. The Maier & Fischer Company acted as both builder and realtor and operated their executive office just west of Kedzie Avenue on 63rd Street. Their actual sales office operated about a mile west, just beyond Crawford (Pulaski) Avenue. Maier & Fischer offered "Fischer-Built" homes with long-term financing and interest rates that were "never over 6 %." The company advertised that it was easy to purchase one of their houses because the huge volume of construction cut costs to a minimum and made possible easy terms to the buyer. Similarly, prominent Polish-American developers William Witwicki and Walery Kozolinski erected bungalows on the 6000 block of South Mozart, offering them for between $7–14,000. Witwicki and Kozolinski purchased 50 lots in southwest suburban Summit on which they planned to erect more bungalows.

While large developers built homes on a grand scale, many bungalows resulted from the individual efforts of craftsmen acting as general contractors to make extra money. In December 1927, John Juszkiewicz of 5521 South May built a home at 2057 West 68th Street designed by architect E.N. Brancher which he planned to sell for $5,000. Juszkiewicz soon took out another permit to build yet another bungalow at 2059 West 68th Place, also offering it for $5,000. Polish and other East European craftsmen and developers entered the Bungalow Belt with an eye on profiting from the housing boom of the 1920s. These more recently arrived immigrant communities saw the 1920s expansion as a chance to live out the American dream. St. Rita's Father Green, concerned about neighborhood stability, had something to say about small developers on the Southwest Side. He complained about "floaters" who built a home and then sold it for only $200 more than they had paid to construct it. Still in the boom times of the late 1920s, bungalow construction meant new families, and new families meant change as well as growth.

Samuel Cardinal Stritch helped the Marquette Park Lithuanian community dedicate this magnificent church on May 12, 1957. Lithuanian folk art and Baroque design influenced architect John Mulokas as he created a distinctly Lithuanian building for the thriving Marquette Park community. (Photograph by Mati Maldre.)

EASTERN EUROPEANS ON THE SOUTHWEST SIDE

One group of immigrant Catholics in particular looked to the Marquette Park area for a chance to create their own community away from both the dirt and noise of the older industrial neighborhoods and from other ethnic groups. Lithuanians saw the Bungalow Belt as a chance to build an ideal ethnic community. In May of 1927, Rev. Alexander Baltutis announced the purchase of 2.5 acres of land at 68th and Washtenaw from Lithuanian Catholic Charities for the creation of a Lithuanian Catholic parish. It was part of a communal effort to build a new community. The $40,000 paid for the land would help the charitable organization build a hospital on an adjacent site. The Sisters of St. Casimir, a Lithuanian order of nuns, had announced that they had intended to build a hospital near Marquette Park the previous November. The Lithuanian community simply recycled money in an attempt to create a presence in the areas to the southwest of its traditional neighborhoods in Bridgeport and Back of the Yards. Their arrival in the Marquette Park/Chicago Lawn neighborhoods emphasized their quick success in the industrial city that they now claimed as home. Father Baltutis' logic was the same as Rev. Green's—if you build ethnic institutions in new areas, you will attract residents to these areas who will feel more secure in entering an area with familiar institutions. Father Baltutis' new parish, the Nativity of the Blessed Virgin Mary, joined an older Lithuanian institution helping to anchor what would be a quickly expanding ethnic community.

Lithuanian Americans organized the Sisters of St. Casimir in 1907 in Pennsylvania. Two years later, the order transferred its motherhouse to Chicago, choosing a site near the newly established Marquette Park for the construction of the order's motherhouse. The sisters arrived in January 1911, and opened St. Casimir Academy as a Lithuanian Catholic school one month later. It enjoyed immediate success, and like St. Rita's attracted families and other institutions to Chicago Lawn's Marquette Park neighborhood. Under the leadership of Mother Marija (Kazimiera Kaupaite), the order's General Superior, the Sisters of St. Casimir expanded their presence across Chicago's Lithuanian community and particularly in Marquette Park.

In 1917, Cardinal Mundelein encouraged the building of a Lithuanian hospital in Chicago. Various Lithuanian organizations responded, raising $400,000 for the construction of Holy Cross Hospital next to the Motherhouse of the Sisters of St. Casimir. The hospital opened on November 9, 1928, just months after the laying of the cornerstone for the new Lithuanian church. Holy Cross Hospital served some 9,000 patients in its first two years of operation. Cardinal Mundelein blessed a combination church and school building for Nativity BVM Church on June 9, 1929. Within 10 years, 800 families belonged to the parish, and the congregation's debt had been paid off. The neighborhood soon became known as the "Lithuanian Gold Coast."

Polish immigrants also made their way out of the older industrial neighborhoods to the Southwest Side's Bungalow Belt, particularly West Lawn. Polish Americans dominated St. Turibius Parish from its origin in 1927. The first pastor, Rev. Thomas Smyk, had served at St. Mary of Perpetual Help parish, a Polish-American congregation, in Bridgeport. It was of course from Bridgeport and the Back of the Yards that most new Polish American residents were migrating into the West Lawn neighborhood. The small congregation first celebrated Mass in the assembly hall of Peck Public School at 59th and Hamlin. Father Smyk soon left and was replaced by Rev. Francis A. Kulinski, who came from St. Joseph's Polish Catholic Parish in Back of the Yards, once again mirroring the movement of Polish Americans across the cityscape. By 1930, 500 parishioners belonged to the congregation, and 145 students attended the parochial school. In 1935, the Sisters of St. Joseph of the Third Order of St. Francis, a Polish order of Catholic nuns organized first in Chicago's Bridgeport neighborhood, opened Lourdes High School in West Lawn. The Polish community established institutional roots in West Lawn on the edge of the prairie.

RACE AND THE SOUTHWEST SIDE BUNGALOW BELT

As Polish, Lithuanian, German, and Irish residents came to the Southwest Side, so did a sizeable Jewish community. In 1928, Dr. E. Charles Sydney came to the Lawn Manor Community Center at 6641 South Troy to serve as rabbi. The arrival of Dr. Sydney caused the rapid growth of the congregation, which saw 200 new members enroll in two months. Despite some feelings of anti-Semitism, Jews too were welcome in the Bungalow Belt. Another group, however, was not. From the beginning, Chicago's strict observance of a racial dividing line between blacks and whites made its presence felt in the Bungalow Belt. During the Great Migration when tens of thousands of African Americans arrived to work in Chicago's industrial plants at the time of World War One, and especially after the 1919 race riot, strict racial segregation was put in place. Race remained as a source of conflict and fear in the city. White residents of all ethnic backgrounds generally agreed with the assumption that the presence of black families meant a neighborhood's decline.

On March 24, 1927, the *Liberty Bell* ran a story titled, "Color Line Scare Stirs 60th Street." Cameron Latter, a Loop attorney, owned some property on West 60th Street just west of the Grand Trunk Railroad tracks. Latter had proposed to build an office and ice delivery station at the site next to a coal yard. The small structure was to be 30-foot by 20-foot and serve as a storage house and office for the delivery of ice. Residents quickly opposed the icehouse idea, claiming that it would mean the constant clatter of horses and delivery wagons along their quiet residential street. Mrs. C.L. Breathwaite of 61st Street led the opposition to the icehouse. Mr. C.F. Keener, who lived across the street from the spot, circulated a petition to prevent construction of the icehouse. Residents argued that the lots had been zoned for bungalows and apartment houses and not industrial purposes. Mr. Latter countered that the site was improperly zoned. The attorney pointed out that a concrete block manufacturing plant currently stood on the land. He then claimed that the Zoning Board of Appeals had already admitted its mistake in zoning the property for residential purposes. In face of the protests, Latter threatened to follow the letter of the law and build three bungalows, but to rent them only to African Americans. This brought more conflict with the community.

Residents wanted neither an icehouse nor blacks in their Bungalow Belt community. A mass meeting was held in April at St. Nicholas of Tolentine Church to protest both Latter's plans for an icehouse or for renting to black families. Mrs. Breathwaite stated that

Margaret Ann Clendenen and her family dressed in their best clothes to attend Easter Mass in 1957, in the Avalon Park neighborhood. (Courtesy of Avis Clendenen.)

The elegantly arched doorway of this Brainerd bungalow frames Dorothy (Driehaus) Mellon's wedding picture on October 10, 1965. (Courtesy of Dorothy Mellon.)

African-American families made their way into the Bungalow Belt in the 1950s and 1960s. Pictured here is Marsha Moseley, standing before the family's Chatham bungalow fireplace on her graduation day from Dixon Elementary School in 1967. (Courtesy of Marsha Moseley.)

while opposed to both plans, she preferred the African-American families to the icehouse. The icehouse was eventually built. The following December, the Southwest Federation of Improvement Clubs met at the Clearing Town Hall at 5635 West 63rd Street. The federation represented neighborhood groups from across Chicago's Southwest Side, including various ethnic organizations. Leaders announced they wanted to prohibit the purchase of property by "colored folks." They called for the imposition of racial covenants on real estate transactions in order to prevent the renting or sale of homes or apartments to African Americans.

Interestingly enough, local Protestant congregations observed Lincoln's birthday by celebrating "Inter-Racial Sunday." In February 1929, the Chicago Lawn Presbyterian Church at 62nd and St. Louis hosted a quartet from Hope Church, an African-American congregation. Rev. A.T. Reading of St. John A.M.E. Church exchanged pulpits with Rev. George B. Drake of Thomas Memorial Congregational Church, a white Chicago Lawn church. The purpose of the exchange was ". . . to foster tolerance and brotherly love and the appreciation of freedom for all men." The *Liberty Bell* hailed the event, calling it one of the most appropriate ways to celebrate the day. The local paper said in its editorial that, "Only by meeting together can the white and colored races ever hope to bring about a better understanding of their problems." Good intentions aside, the realities of racial prejudice in Chicago remained difficult to confront. Events in the 1930s and 1940s, however, would cause pressures across the city and suburbs eventually bringing change to the Bungalow Belt. First the Great Depression and then the Second World War brought a halt to bungalow construction. The post-1945 era saw the revitalization of residential construction, especially in outlying neighborhoods and suburbs. But tastes had changed and more modern looking buildings appeared on the side streets of the city. Developers now built Cape Cods and Raised Ranches as they filled in the empty land left after the bungalow explosion of the 1920s. The result was a more diverse series of bungalow neighborhoods.

CHANGE AND THE BUNGALOW BELT

The Bungalow Belt had always symbolized upward mobility and middle-class status for Chicagoans. Home ownership, neat lawns, steady jobs, a fine education for children, consumer goods, especially an automobile, and a particularly intense American patriotism has long been identified with the city's outlying neighborhoods. Bungalow Belt families prided themselves on their middle-class values. As early as 1927, the Chicago Lawn State Bank urged families to save for their son's college education. This spoke directly to the aspirations of residents who saw their children's future as limitless at a time when a college education was still rare among the ethnic middle class. Like most Chicagoans, they generally voted Democratic, but they tended to identify with the more conservative wing of the party. Residents supported labor unions but hoped to move into the professional class. Bungalow Belt politics meant support for organized labor, good city services, religion, and the racial status quo.

In the 15 years after World War II, Chicago's housing stock grew rapidly. Builders erected over 600,000 housing units in the Chicago area, mostly in outlying neighborhoods and in the suburbs. Following Chicago's racial tradition, these areas did not welcome African Americans. Blacks with middle-class hopes had few choices. The outlying housing boom did, however, attract whites living in older neighborhoods, including many in the Bungalow Belt. The result was the freeing up of neighborhoods closer in to the original industrial core for the African American market.

Parts of the South Side's Bungalow Belt saw change in the 1950s and 1960s. Chatham located to the south of 79th Street and east of Parnell to the Illinois Central Railroad tracks witnessed bungalow construction in the 1920s. The community area saw its population jump from 9,774 at the beginning of the decade to over 36,000 in 1930. The population stood as 99.7 percent white that year. Racial change came in the 1950s, and by 1960, blacks made up more than 63 percent of the area's population. Segregation was almost complete 10 years later. Chatham remained a middle-class community. Headquarters of various large African American-owned businesses located in Chatham. Many of Chicago's most successful black families put down roots in the neighborhood. Obviously black families also looked to the Bungalow Belt, which with the exception of a small section of Morgan Park had been restricted to them, for upward mobility and the American Dream of home ownership. Chatham and then other sections of the South Side opened up this possibility in the post-war era, despite the continuing cycle of segregation, temporary integration, and resegregation in Chicago.

Racial change spread quickly across the city. South Shore, Grand Crossing, and Avalon Park all witnessed change and turmoil. To the east of Chicago Lawn, first Englewood and then West Englewood neighborhoods witnessed quick racial turnover. Still as late as 1970, no African Americans lived in Chicago Lawn, West Lawn, or Gage Park. This despite the fact that four years earlier Dr. Martin Luther King Jr. led an open housing march into Gage Park and Chicago Lawn (Marquette Park). This march, and later ones in the 1960s and 1970s, led to violence. White youths rioted, stoning and sometimes burning the cars of innocent Chicagoans passing through the district. Rioters unfurled the flags of the Confederacy and of the American Nazi Party in Marquette Park. Police in riot gear patrolled the district. Marquette Park, Gage Park, and the entire Southwest Side became national symbols of Northern racism.

After 1980, however, racial integration arrived in both Gage Park and Marquette Park. African Americans, Hispanics, Asians, and Arab Americans joined the diverse group of Euro-ethnics in this neighborhood some 7 miles southwest of the Loop. According to the 1990 census, blacks made up 26.6 percent of the population of Chicago Lawn, while Hispanics made up 28.4 percent of the community area's 51,243 residents. In Gage Park just to the north, Hispanics made up 39.2 percent of the population, blacks only 5.1percent, and whites 54.9 percent—a drop of 31 percent from 1980, while the population grew 10.3 percent. A look at the breakdown of the various white ethnic groups in Chicago Lawn and Gage Park shows the ethnic diversity of these two communities. According to the 1990 census in which an ethnic ancestry question was posed, the Irish made up the largest European ethnic group in Chicago Lawn with 7.6 percent of the population. They were followed in turn by the Lithuanians and Poles, each with 6.7 percent of the residents of the community area. All three Euro-ethnic groups stood far

These Cape Cod houses built after World War II represented a new generation of houses in the Marquette Park neighborhood. Built on land just to the south of the park not developed during the bungalow era, they continued the tradition of single-family detached homes with a simple floor plan.

The Nabisco Bakery dominates the neighborhood's skyline, again connecting these Cape Cods to their working-class forerunners. (Photograph by Mati Maldre.)

behind the Mexicans, who made up 22.7percent of the population. Other Hispanics, especially Puerto Ricans, explain the larger Hispanic number listed in the census.

In Gage Park, where Mexicans account for 32.7 percent of the residential population, Poles provided the second largest group with 18.0 percent in 1990. They were followed by the Irish (9.2 percent) and the Germans (8.5 percent). A substantial Middle Eastern population, largely Palestinian, was also centered in both Chicago Lawn and Gage Park. In West Lawn and West Elsdon, just to the west the demographic character of these areas did not shift as much as the areas to the east. In 1990, West Lawn whites made up 88.2 percent of the population. Among these Euro-ethnics, the Poles lead with 29.1 percent of the population. The Irish followed with 15.8 percent. Behind them were Germans (12.9 percent) and Italians (8.1 percent). Mexicans actually made up the fourth largest group in West Lawn, with 8.9 percent of the population. While Hispanic growth by 1990 had not been as great in West Lawn as in the community areas to the east, it obviously grew especially in that part of West Lawn to the east of Pulaski Avenue. In 1990, Hispanics accounted for over 10 percent of the overall West Lawn population.

The trends of the 1980s continued into the 1990s. Chicago Lawn and Gage Park are today largely Hispanic and African American neighborhoods. Still, a large number of white ethnics and their institutions remain in the district. The opening of the CTA's Orange Line, connecting the Southwest Side's Midway Airport with the Loop in the 1990s, resulted in increased land values and brought new investment to the area. Father Green's St. Rita's Church today offers Mass in Spanish as well as in English. As in the 1920s, school populations are growing. Most of the new children are black or Hispanic as a new generation begins to yet again redefine the city's Bungalow Belt. Chicago's bungalows remain symbols of upward mobility and even change 80 years after their construction in a wide belt across the city.

seven

THE PEOPLE OF THE
BUNGALOW BELT, 2001

by Harry Meyer

Anthony Lo Bue and his wife, Diane Moss, stand beside their Marquette Park bungalow. The bungalow features some very unique leaded art glass windows, but the gargoyle, a later addition, generally catches the eye first.

My task was to take photographs of bungalows and their occupants all across the city. I traveled from my new home (not a bungalow) on the extreme south side of the city, 11500 South to be exact, all the way to Touhy Avenue, 7000 North. Traveling along the Bungalow Belt, I stopped for a closer look in the communities of Beverly, South Shore, Marquette Park, Chicago Lawn, Portage Park, Galewood, Mayfair, Jefferson Park, Ravenswood Gardens, and finally West Rogers Park.

The people that live in bungalows are as diverse as the bungalows in which they live. Twenty images can only begin to demonstrate that diversity. The bungalows ranged from elaborate to common. Many had art glass or built-in features, while others had neither. Probably the most common feature was the built in faux fireplace. Unifying attributes though were the solid construction and practical/adaptable floor plans. Standup attics and full basements add to the adaptability and often turned a two-bedroom home into one with four or five. The full basements, a Chicago tradition, were places for family gatherings or used to cook in or otherwise escape the summer heat in pre-air conditioned days.

Many of the people that agreed to be photographed talked of "restoring" their homes. They found interesting features buried in walls, hidden away in attics, or lost in years of paint. One found French doors that had been covered over on both sides, while another found beautiful leaded glass doors lost in the attic. New owners wondered how hard it would be to remove years of paint from fireplaces, cabinets, and woodwork.

So how were the people? They were great, each with a different story. Their homes reflected their individuality. The Syed house reflected Ahmed's Indian/Pakistani lineage; the Sofilj's Eastern European background; Iris May's, her family photo display; Amy and Judy's home, an assemblage of things collected. Some had spent nearly all their lives in their bungalow while others were very new, including one who was just moving in. Many had been drawn to the bungalow because of its utilitarian but elegant style.

A final note about neighborhoods. I was surprised at how well the communities along the belt are doing. Beverly, long held up as an inclusive community, was indeed that, but so were Galewood, West Rogers Park, Ravenswood Gardens, and of all places, Marquette Park. It's not scientific, but it seems there is a connection between the good people of the Bungalow Belt and the good communities they live in.

Ahmed Syed and his wife, Marcia Hermansen, are pictured at their West Rogers Park home. The interior of the home is decorated with rugs, furniture, and other items, giving it a distinctive Indian/Pakistani feel. The word bungalow is derived from the Hindi word bangla, *a small airy home common to the eastern part of the Indian subcontinent.*

Iris May, a former schoolteacher, enjoys her "front" room with nicely leaded glass windows and part of her collection of family photos displayed along the covered radiator. Ms. May has lived in South Shore since 1967.

Memory Jacobs and her daughters, Mia and Mira, live in the East Beverly neighborhood. The mantel above their faux fireplace is their favorite place for the family photo gallery. The Jacobs have lived at this address for about two years.

Jan Boden is shown in front of her home, which is next door to the Jacobs. She has lived here for more than seven years and shares her home with her buddy Grommet, a Border collie. Jan's bungalow is a reflective image of her neighbor's.

Amy Cornell and Judy Delvoye live in Portage Park. They enjoy decorating their home with antiques and items purchased at garage sales.

The Gerald Hollowells family has lived in the Chicago Lawn community for about five years. Shortly after purchasing their bungalow, they joined the Southwest Home Equity Assurance Program, which guarantees the value of their home if they live there for five years.

Sandra and Borivoje Sofilj emigrated from Bosnia. They have lived in their bungalow in the Mayfair neighborhood for about three years.

Roberto and Elia Cruz have lived in their Chicago Lawn home for eight years.

The Sera family live on North Kildare Street in Chicago. They had just returned from son Brian's T-ball game.

The Cardenas family moved to Chicago from Waukegan about six years ago and purchased a bungalow in the North Mayfair neighborhood. Lilla Cardenas and her daughter, Camille, are pictured here making a homemade piñata in their backyard.

Martha and Michael Johnston live with their children in West Lawn. A previous owner had rented out rooms to flight personnel from Midway Airport. The Johnstons have lived there for only two years.

Anibal Malave and his wife, Sonia, are pictured in their Marquette Manor home. Anibal was one of the first Puerto Rican residents in Southwest Chicago. He has lived on the Southwest Side for about 30 years and in this home for roughly 15 years.

Bob and Meaghan Newton are expecting the arrival of their first child later this summer. They have lived in the North Mayfair community for about two years.

Dale Bolling has lived in her North Tripp home for 73 years. She grew up there and was able to remain in the bungalow after getting married. During the Great Depression, she recalled that they rented out both the attic and basement to help pay the mortgage. Dale has been an active leader in the North River Commission community organization. Her husband, Hans, who was a commercial artist, finished their basement himself.

Kenneth Arrizola, Miki, and their two sons live in a Ravenswood Garden bungalow. Ken is a project manager for an architectural firm. He bought the home while single as a "great bachelor pad." Soon he met Miki and started a family.

Mary and Abdula Falaah-U-Deen live on the 64th and Fairfield Model Bungalow Block. They have lived in this home for about seven years and were concerned about the five nearby abandoned houses. They now have new enthusiasm for a rebirth of the block; the City of Chicago's Department of Housing declared it their Model Bungalow Block. The five abandoned homes will be completely rehabbed and resold by the end of 2001.

Jovencio Constantino and his son, Hunter, are proud of their Jefferson Park home with its ornate brickwork and leaded glass windows.

Jan and Carleen Lorys have lived in their West Rogers Park bungalow for 17 years. Jan is director of the Polish Museum of America, and Carleen works in the public school system.

Bill Chin, Xan Nelson, and their family live in West Rogers Park. Bill is a musician and does a lot of work out of his home. Bill and Xan bought the house about 15 years ago and soon after had their first child, Julian.

Cindy and Pat Malloy have lived in their Beverly home for over 27 years. Many members of the Malloy's extended family also live in bungalows nearby. Mayor Richard M. Daley announced the City of Chicago's Bungalow Initiative in front of the Malloy bungalow in the fall of 2000.

SUGGESTED READING

Brierton, Joan M., *American Restoration Style*, (2000).

Bigott, Joseph C., *From Cottage To Bungalow, Houses and the Working Class in Metropolitan Chicago, 1869-1929*, (2001).

Blaszcyk, Regina Lee, *Imagining Consumers: Design and Innovation from Wedgwood to Corning*, (2000).

Cigliano, Jan, *American Restoration Style: Bungalow* (1998).

Commission on Chicago Landmarks and the Chicago Department of Planning and Development. *Chicago Historic Resources Survey: An Inventory of Architecturally and Historically Significant Structures*. (1996).

Duchsherer, Paul and Douglas Keister, *The Bungalow: America's Arts and Crafts Home*, (1995);

—— *Inside the Bungalow: America's Arts and Crafts Interior*, (1997)

—— *Outside the Bungalow: America's Arts and Crafts Garden*, (1999).

Fitch, James Marston, *American Building: The Historical Forces that Shaped It* second edition (1968).

Friedman, Alice T., *Women and the Making of the Modern House* (1998).

Hitchmough, Wendy, *The Arts and Crafts Lifestyle and Design*, (2000).

Hoyt, Homer, *One Hundred Years of Land Values in Chicago* (1933).

Hunter, Christine, *Ranches, Rowhouses, and Railroad Flats* (1999).

King, Anthony D., *The Bungalow: The Production of a Global Culture* (1995).

Lancaster, Clay, *The American Bungalow, 1880-1930* (1995).

McAlester, Virginia and Lee, *A Field Guide to American Houses* (1997).

Matthews, Mary Lockwood, *The House and its Care* (1929).

Mayer, Harold M. and Richard C. Wade, *Chicago: Growth of a Metropolis* (1969).

Monchow, Helen, *Seventy Years of Real Estate Subdividing in the Region of Chicago* (1931).

Pacyga, Dominic A. and Ellen Skerrett, *Chicago: City of Neighborhoods* (1986).

Rybczynski, Witold, *Looking Around* (1992).

Sanders, Barry, *A Complex Fate: Gustav Stickley and the Craftsman Movement* (1996).

Sears, Roebuck and Company, *Honor Built Modern Homes*, (1926) reprint edition Sears, Roebuck and Company, *Sears, Roebuck Catalog Of Houses, 1926*, (1991).

Stern, Marc Jeffery, *The Pottery Industry Of Trenton: A Skilled Trade in Transition, 1850-1929*, (1994).

Stevenson, Katherine Cole and H. Ward Jandl, *Houses by Mail: A Guide to Houses from Sears, Roebuck and Company* (1996).

Turgeon, Kitty, and Robert Rust, *The Arts&Crafts Home* (1998).

Valetin von Hoist, Herman, *Country and Suburban Homes of the Prairie School Period*, (1982).

Winter, Robert and Alexander Vertikoff, *American Bungalow Style* (1996).

Wright, Gwendolyn, *Moralism and the Modern Home* (1980).

——— *Building the Dream* (1998).

Acknowledgments

Many people and institutions have come together to make both this book and the Chicago Architecture Foundation's exhibition, "The Chicago Bungalow," possible. Special thanks goes to John G. Markowski, Commissioner, City of Chicago Department of Housing; the Richard H. Driehaus Foundation; the Illinois Humanities Council; the Graham Foundation; the National Endowment for the Arts; and the Elizabeth F. Cheney Foundation. The Conrad Sulzer Regional Library, Woodson Regional Library, Downer's Grove Historical Society, Beverly Arts Center, Park Ridge Library, Polish Museum of America, Czechoslovak Heritage Museum, Balzekas Museum of Lithuanian Culture, Chicago Lawn Historical Society, and the Rogers Park Historical Society have all provided advice and help to this project.

Robert Brugemann provided counsel as both the book and exhibition projects began to be formulated. He met with the various contributors to this volume and several staff members of the Chicago Architecture Foundation (CAF) at a memorable luncheon at the Cliff Dwellers Club in October 2000, to help clarify the major themes explored in the project. Stacey Stearn worked long hours writing grant proposals. David Laney and Donna Cicinelli aided in preparation of the illustrations for the book. Christine Esposito helped publicize the bungalow exhibit and book projects, making it possible to collect sources hidden away in Chicago's neighborhoods. A special thanks goes to Glen Humphreys of Chicago's Sulzer Regional Library and Andrea Telli and the staff of the Special Collections and Preservation Division of the Chicago Public Library. John Kimbrough of the John Crerar Library made rare copies of the *American Builder* available to the editors. Tim Samuelson of the Chicago Historical Society gave us important insights into the history of Chicago's residential architecture. James Vondrak and the staff of the *Southwest News-Herald* made available copies of the *Liberty Bell*. Michael Williams proved to be an invaluable guide to housing in the Rogers Park/West Ridge area. Chicago Lawn historian Kathy Headley helped find rare photographs of that community. Lisa Roberts, Director of the Garfield Park Conservatory, provided information about landscaping styles of the period. Ellen Skerrett, one of the book's contributors, also helped find photographs, sources, and provided support in many ways. David Chowliak, Tom Drebenstedt, and Dick Spurgin helped to create a series of CAF tours and added information and insights to the research that went behind both the book and exhibit.

None of this would have been possible without the support of Lynn Osmond, President of the Chicago Architecture Foundation. Bonita Mall, Vice President of the Chicago Architecture Foundation, invited Dominic Pacyga to curate the exhibit and inspired this accompanying book. Without her energy, humor, and friendship neither the book nor the exhibit would have been realized. Zurich Esposito's calmness and ability to get things done proved to be priceless. The staff of the Chicago Architecture Foundation performed their usual magic.

Many Chicagoans gave of their time, photographs, and memories. They are too numerous to mention by name, but a heartfelt thanks goes out to them. Bungalow Belt residents allowed Mati Maldre and Harry Meyer into their homes to document buildings and families. Their pride in their bungalows and manicured lawns were obvious. This book belongs to them.

Finally, Dominic Pacyga wishes to thank Kathleen Alaimo, Johanna and Beatrice Pacyga, and numerous friends and confidants for listening to bungalow talk for the past two years. Charles Shanabruch thanks Patricia Bryant, Thomas and Stephen Shanabruch, Steven Murphy, August Kolich, and Alderman Virginia Rugai for giving their ears and nurturing ideas about Chicago's Bungalow Belt.

Dominic A. Pacyga
Charles Shanabruch

CONTRIBUTORS

JOSEPH C. BIGOTT is an Assistant Professor in the Department of History and Political Science at Purdue University Calumet. He is the author of *From Cottage To Bungalow: Houses and the Working Class in Metropolitan Chicago 1869 to 1929*.

JAN CIGLIANO, an architectural historian, is an editor with Princeton Architectural Press in New York. She is the author of five books, including *Bungalow: American Restoration Style, Private Washington: Residences in the Nation's Capital, Showplace of America: Cleveland's Euclid Avenue, and Grand American Avenue, 1850-1920*.

MATI MALDRE, a professor of photography/art at Chicago State University, has exhibited his photographs widely in the United States and abroad. He has specialized in the photography of residential architecture and is the author of *Griffin in America*.

HARRY MEYER is a freelance photographer who has lived in the middle of the Bungalow Belt (nearly) all his life. He is also Director of Commercial Development at Greater SW Development Corporation, a nonprofit community development organization located in the Marquette Park Community.

ELLEN SKERRETT is a research scholar with the University of Illinois at Chicago on the project examining Hull House and its neighborhood in the early twentieth century. She is editor of *At the Crossroads: Old Saint Patrick's and the Chicago Irish* and co-author of *Chicago: City of Neighborhoods; The Irish in Chicago; and Catholicism, Chicago Style*.

SCOTT SONOC, AIA, is President of Sonoc Architects & Associates and consultant to the Historic Chicago Bungalow Initiative. He earned a Masters in Architecture from the University of Illinois, Chicago, and a Bachelors in Design from Illinois Institute of Technology, and has worked for the City of Chicago, Murphy/Jahn Inc., and Solomon Cordwell Buenz & Associates.